How to Start a Small Business in 2020

10,000/Month Ultimate Guide - From Business Idea and Plan to Marketing and Scaling, including Funding Strategies, Legal Structure, and Administration Tips

By

Ronald Robert

© **Copyright 2019 – Ronald Roberts - All rights reserved.**

The content contained within this book may not be reproduced, duplicated or transmitted without direct written permission from the author or the publisher.

Under no circumstances will any blame or legal responsibility be held against the publisher, or author, for any damages, reparation, or monetary loss due to the information contained within this book. Either directly or indirectly.

Legal Notice:

This book is copyright protected. This book is only for personal use. You cannot amend, distribute, sell, use, quote or paraphrase any part, or the content within this book, without the consent of the author or publisher.

Disclaimer Notice:

Please note the information contained within this document is for educational and entertainment purposes only. All effort has been executed to present accurate, up to date, and reliable, complete information. No warranties of any kind are declared or implied. Readers acknowledge that the author is not engaging in the rendering of legal, financial, medical or professional advice. The content within this book has been derived from various sources. Please consult a licensed professional before attempting any techniques outlined in this book.

By reading this document, the reader agrees that under no circumstances is the author responsible for any losses, direct or indirect, which are incurred as a result of the use of information contained within this document, including, but not limited to, — errors, omissions, or inaccuracies.

Table of Contents

Chapter 1: The Basics of Getting Started 6

Chapter 2: Creating a Workable and Winning Business Plan 14

Chapter 3: Choosing a Legal Structure 24

Chapter 4: Getting Funding for Your Business ... 34

Chapter 5: Marketing your Business Effectively. 43

Chapter 6: Effective Administration Tips for Small Businesses 54

Chapter 7: Why Small Businesses Fail in the First Year 63

Chapter 8: Surviving Your First Year in Business 72

Chapter 9: Scaling your Business 80

Chapter 10: Best Practices for Small Businesses 88

Chapter 11: Essential Soft Skills for Successful Entrepreneurs 100

Conclusion 110

References 112

Chapter 1: The Basics of Getting Started

Many people dream of being business owners. There's an apparent allure to being your own boss, changing the lives of others while making money and charting the course of your life and fortune. Unfortunately, very few ever actualize this dream. For most, it remains a distant daydream that comes alive when the boss is being unbearable, or when the paycheck is stretched thin by what seems like a million bills. Whether you are employed or in between jobs, you can turn your life around with just a dream and a strategy. That is how most businesses start and it is definitely how many fortunes have been made.

The truth is that while many people wish they could run their own businesses, very few know where to begin. Starting a business can be exceptionally daunting, especially when there are naysayers at every corner bombarding you with stories of failure. It is even worse when you have a job which you are considering leaving to start your own business. You'll find yourself having to deal with a lot of criticism for this less-than-ideal decision. How dare you leave the comfort and stability of a regular paycheck to chase the pipe dream of entrepreneurship? If you are doubting your ability to become and thrive as an entrepreneur, it should comfort you to know that everyone has the potential to become an entrepreneur. There are over seven billion people on earth and every one of them has the ability to create something and sell it for profit. You might not succeed immediately, as many successful entrepreneurs have learned, but there is profit in commitment.

Every good entrepreneur begins their journey with a vision.

Merriam-Webster dictionary defines vision as 'a thought, concept or object formed by the imagination'. As an entrepreneur, your vision has everything to do with what you hope to see your business evolve into in the long term. This vision will serve as the guiding light in your entrepreneurial journey, always reminding you of why you got started and what waits on the other side of hard work and commitment. Your vision is what you will sell to potential investors and yourself on those days when you feel like quitting. But not so fast--if a vision is powerful, a verified vision is even more so. Verifying your vision means checking to see whether the idea in your mind is something that can take off in the real world. Often times, even the most brilliant ideas are not ready for launch yet. A wise person once said that nothing can stop an idea whose time has come. As a hopeful business owner, you have to ascertain that your idea's time has come, because the goal is to be unstoppable. Research, networking, and piloting are all great ways to go about verifying your vision. You should never get started on a business until you are confident that you have used all sounding boards at your disposal and found it to be worth the investment.

So, what happens when you want to start a business but don't have a vision yet? How do you proceed from this quagmire? The process of arriving at a vision is not a one-day affair. For some lucky people, it will be a light-bulb moment where they encounter an inconvenience that they feel they can solve for everyone else, at a profit. For others, the development of a vision is a journey of many months and years. You will not be able to sit in your living room and command a vision to come to you. Sometimes, you'll be required to seek some inspiration. Entrepreneurship events, seminars led by established business persons, publications, TED Talks, and online tutorials are places you can look to for inspiration. Going about life while alert to the opportunities presented by everyday transactions and interactions is yet another way to find your vision. Trusting the process is one major ingredient of arriving at an actionable vision.

Once you are armed with a verified vision, you can proceed to look into whether you have everything else that is required when starting up a business.

Business Name and Legal Structure

If you thought choosing a name for your kid was hard, try choosing one for your business! Unlike kids, where you can name yours Madison even though there are several Madisons down the block, business names are protected by copyright laws. You cannot choose a name that is already in existence, however appropriate it seems for your business. Choosing the right business name for your company can make a whole lot of difference for your brand. A good business name should communicate the value and promise of your brand. It should be memorable and not ambiguous. It is not mandatory that your business name carries an exact description of your products or services. In fact, a seemingly non-informative name can carry your brand to success if it is followed up with a thorough and solid marketing plan. Stay away from names which are puns, as the joke might be lost on your audience. If you have a catchy phrase that you are considering as a business name or tagline, do your homework to ensure it is not offensive in particular regions. This can be especially awkward should you decide to expand into said regions. Car manufacturers know this probably better than anyone else. For instance, the Mitsubishi Pajero had to be renamed to Montero for the

Spanish market so that it could be more acceptable. While the Pajero was initially named after a pampas cat (Leopardus pajeros) it turned out that the name meant something entirely different in Spanish-speaking regions.

Your business' legal structure is the other item that you should check off the list. Chapter 2 delves deep into the different legal structures and the considerations you should make before settling on one.

Business Plan

A business plan is a document that will be useful for you as a business owner, and potential investors as well. A business plan clearly articulates the direction of your business and demonstrates your knowledge in your market of operation. It is a document that will come in handy when you want to remind yourself of what is at stake and show investors what value you propose to bring to the market. If your business plan is created well, it can be leveraged to win you all the rewards you wish for as a new business owner. Chapter 1 focuses on the business plan and provides tips on how to go about creating a winning business plan for your new company.

Permits and Licenses

Most jurisdictions require business owners to obtain various permits and licenses before they can be allowed to operate a business. The specific type of permits required vary depending on the type of business you will be operating. For instance, if you wish to open a restaurant, you will be required to have a food service license, which is not necessary if you intend to open a bookstore. Generally, the permits and licenses needed for most businesses include a business license, which allows you to run a business in your particular city. You might also require a fire department license if you will have physical premises that are open to the public and an air and water pollution control permit, especially if your work involves discharge of waste materials. It is important to check with your city's council offices for a comprehensive list of permits and licenses that are mandatory for all business owners, and for your particular type of business.

Employees

If your business is relatively small, you might be able to run it as a one-person show. However, most businesses will require at least one helping hand to ensure that operations are smooth and uninterrupted. Before you open your business to the public, ensure that you have the right team on board to help you take care of day-to-day tasks. A team could be composed of permanent employees or consultants and freelancers who are available on a need basis. In the beginning of your business, you might want to outsource as much of the work as possible instead of hiring permanent employees. This way, you can cut down on start-up costs, as hiring full-time employees is likely to cost you a lot more than pushing work to a freelancer would. Either way, you'll need to know that you have people who will help you implement your company's vision. If you are selling a product that will be dispatched to customers within your city, have a delivery service or at least one delivery guy on stand-by. If you intend to engage with your customers on social media, get a social media manager on board to interact with online customers when you are up and about looking for investors. Assemble the right team early on and be clear about their roles and job descriptions. Once your company is up and running, you'll be glad that you have one less thing to worry about because someone else is worrying about it.

Business Insurance

This is not something you want to think about when starting your business, but things actually do go wrong at the most unexpected of times. If and when this happens, it helps to have insurance to cover you for any losses incurred. For a small business, general liability and property insurance are ideal. General liability insurance, sometimes referred to as business liability insurance, protects you from claims that arise from your business operations. These claims could range from bodily injury to personal injury and even property damage. If customers lodge complaints that they have suffered any harm from your products or services, you can use funds from your general liability insurance to settle the costs of the claims. On the other hand, property insurance protects you in the event that your business premises are damaged, or the contents of the premises are stolen. Property insurance includes homeowners' insurance, which means you can still insure your business property even if your company is based in your home.

Branding

Once you have gotten all your ducks in a row in terms of a business name, plan, and business permits and licenses, you should embark on creating an identity for your business. Do not just tell people about your company - show them too. A well-done logo and business website will do wonders when it comes to pushing your business out there. Hire a good designer and printer to create some professional business cards for you, that you can hand out at networking events and to potential customers. Invest in promotional material such as brochures and flyers as well. While your marketing efforts will involve a little more than printed material, it is still a good place to start as far as establishing a presence within your community is concerned.

Commitment to the Cause

This is not something that you can buy off a shelf, but it is definitely a key item to have before you start your business. Commitment can be defined as faithfulness to a cause or activity. It is the sheer dedication that will take you through the tough days before you even break even. Commitment calls for you to be loyal to your vision even when everyone else is doubting it, one year after you have set up shop. There are various ways you can use to check whether you really are committed, and therefore ready, to start your small business. These include determining what you are willing to give up to get started. If you are interested in starting a business but are still excited about the prospect of getting a paycheck from your current employer, you are probably not too committed to entrepreneurship. It does not mean that everyone must quit their job to start a business, but it is a little difficult to give one hundred percent to your new company when your employer expects the very same at work. The math just doesn't look right.

A Good Network

During the first year of business, you will be very grateful for the people you know because they will play a big role in getting you your first customer. Your network of family, friends, and colleagues is vital to marketing your business (and even getting you investors) so make sure you are building the right relationships. Keep in mind that the best time to build a relationship is when you do not need it. Many business owners make the mistake of trying to be friends with a potential investor or mentor when they desperately need them. This approach only makes the person feel used. After all, everyone is human and there needs to be some level of appreciation for the human they are and not the things they can provide. Focus on building strong, genuine relationships with the people you come across that are strong-willed and positive-minded. Take them out for lunch. Meet them for drinks after work. You will be so grateful you surrounded yourself with the right people when you start your business and start to see their input trickling in.

Chapter 2: Creating a Workable and Winning Business Plan

A business plan is one of the most important documents that you can create for your business. A business plan outlines your company's goals and objectives, and the steps you'll take to achieving these objectives. The timeframe within which these business goals must be attained is also documented. Your company's business plan will serve as your roadmap for success, detailing what needs to be done and when. This plan will also come in handy when you need to look back and evaluate whether you are on the right track. If you are in the market for a lender, a business plan will come in hand in convincing your preferred bank that your business idea is worth a business loan.

Many entrepreneurs will set off without a business plan, simply because they find the process of creating one tedious and overwhelming. It can be especially discouraging to create a business plan only for it to become outdated in the face of a dynamic business environment. The good news is that you do not have to spend months working on a business plan, however ideal and thorough this might be. If writing is not your forte, you can hire a consultant to create a business plan for you. For this to work well, you will need to do the research yourself and hand over the information to the writer. Alternatively, you can download a business plan template and customize it to suit your business idea. There are thousands of freely available online templates that are easily accessible through a simple Internet search. Whether you outsource the creation of your business plan or undertake it yourself, it is important to be mindful of the key components of a business plan. These include the executive summary, business description, product or service description, market analysis, organization and management, sales strategies, funding requirements, and financial projections.

Executive Summary

The executive summary of your business plan is your elevator pitch and summarizes all the key points of the other sections of your business plan. The executive summary should clearly communicate your value proposition to your audience. In many cases, potential investors will only look at the executive summary of your business plan before deciding whether you are worth the investment or not. For this reason, the executive summary is commonly considered the most important part of your business plan. It is recommended that you write the executive summary last after the other sections of the business plan so that these other sections can inform the content of the summary. Many executive summaries are only a page long. If your executive summary is longer than this, it is still okay as long as it does not go beyond 10% of the entire business plan. The best executive summary is one that stays below the 5% threshold. For instance, if your entire business plan is 50 pages long, an ideal executive summary would be 5% of 50 pages which comes to two and a half pages.

Business Description

While the executive summary provides a teaser of what your business is all about, the business description goes into details of your business and the business model. The business description should include details about your company's inception and the mission statement. These are vital in communicating the origins of your company, and the noble reasons behind its beginnings. Describing your business allows your audience to connect with your brand and the person behind the brand. It gives a sneak peek into your business and allows your business to tell its story.

There are several other questions that you should answer in the business description. These include:

- What is the name of your business?
- What services or products do you provide?
- Who are your target customers?
- What is your competitive advantage?
- Since when have you been in business?
- Who are the owners and decision makers of your company?
- What is your legal structure-are you a sole proprietorship, a partnership, etc.?
- Where is your business located?

Market Analysis

A market analysis is a quantitative and qualitative review of your target market. A market analysis is intended to show your potential investors that you understand your market and that this market is big enough to allow sustainable business. In order to present an in-depth market analysis, you will be required to look into the demographics, market need, customer segmentation, barriers to entry, regulations and your competition. The demographics of a market refers to the data of a population that relates to their characteristics such as race, income level, age, education, occupation, and even gender. This is important information that you'll need to find out about your target market. If you know that your target market is made up of college-educated white males in their thirties, then you can tailor your product to fit their very specific needs. Customer segmentation is the process of arranging your customer base by their demographic characteristics. This division happens so that you can correctly tailor your marketing message in a way that resonates with customers best.

Often, the investors you approach will usually have an idea of what your intended target market is like. After all, when you are an investor these are the things you are required to know. If you demonstrate that you know even more than the investor, you will stand a better chance of getting investment capital. At the same time, you want to know your market better for your own sake, so that you do not get nasty surprises along the way.

Organizational Structure and Management

In this section of the business plan, you should highlight all the qualities, skills, and expertise of your management team. In many cases, investors will be looking to see who will be on board before investing. The investors need to know that you have assembled a team that can stick it out to the bitter end and give them value for their investment. Make sure to highlight each and every relevant qualification, however unnecessary it might look to you. An investor might be drawn to put their money in a project if your chief accountant shares their passion for charitable work and fundraising. Sometimes, you really cannot tell with these investors. You just need to put your best foot forward.

If your business is going to be a sole proprietorship, use the limelight provided by this section to show why you are worthy of a second look and an investment. Talk about your educational qualifications, industry expertise, publications and anything else that would grab attention. The organizational structure and management section should not be anything other than impressive.

Marketing and Sales Strategies

So far, your business plan has managed to convince its audience of the value of your intended product or service, your understanding of the market you'll be playing in, and the human resources who will implement your vision. There's still one thing that investors will be looking to find out: the how. The sales strategy section of the business plan will delve into detailing how you intend to price your product, and how this will tie in with other company numbers.

In this section, you will be required to explain your pricing strategy and should be able to explain why you chose that particular strategy. As a business owner, there are some tried and tested pricing strategies that you can use to determine the cost of your product or service. One of these strategies is referred to as penetration pricing, which is a strategy that involves pricing your product low to attract customers in a competitive market, and then raising the price later when you've gained traction.

Value-based pricing is another pricing strategy that you can consider. Value-based pricing usually involves pricing your product by estimating how much a customer would be willing to pay for it. In short, the price of your product answers the question: how much value does a customer see in this product? If the answer is high, the price can be set as high as you wish. Value-based pricing works best when you are operating in a niche market, such as high-end fashion or when there is a shortage and customers are willing to pay higher for a product or service. Unless you are truly and positively convinced that your product or service is exclusive and highly sought after, you might want to avoid value-based pricing. At least until you have gained loyal customers.

Cost-plus pricing is a simple pricing strategy that involves adding a markup to the costs of producing one unit and then setting that as the price. Most new businesses will prefer to go for cost-plus pricing as it is simple and straightforward. Competitive pricing, on the other hand, involves looking at what your competitors are offering and setting a price that can compete in the same market. If you are about to launch a business that is offering a product that has been in the market for a long time, and that is offered by multiple outlets, you might want to try out competitive pricing.

Other than the pricing strategies, you'll also want to include information on activities that you are undertaking to promote brand awareness. You should include information on already completed, ongoing, and future activities. You will also be required to provide information on where you intend to sell your product or service, and how these will be distributed. If you are a sole proprietorship, you should include a detailed plan of how you intend to sell your product on your own. If you will be outsourcing the sales work to a marketing company or sales team, make sure to mention this. If your company will have a permanent sales team, you can reiterate this information even though you had highlighted it in the Organizational Structure and

Management section.

Funding Requirements

By this point, you've told potential investors almost everything they need to know about you, your vision and passion, your product, excellent team, and sales strategy. Investors will usually know by now if you have thought through your plan and if you are worth investing in. Still, there's one piece of information you have yet to provide, and that is how much money you are asking for.

If you have ever watched the TV Show Shark Tank, you may have noticed how some entrepreneurs ask for ridiculous amounts of capital in exchange for a certain percentage of shares, without a full understanding of what informed this amount. The typical outcome is that the entrepreneur is left with a blank look of cluelessness on his face while the Sharks send him on his merry way. If only they had taken the time to understand how much capital they were asking for, and why…

The amount of money you seek as venture capital can discredit your entire business plan, especially if you are unrealistic about it. The process of correctly determining your funding requirements should be preceded by thorough math and basic accounting.

First, you'll need to have your financial numbers well laid out in a manner that shows your expected costs, the financial resources you have to cover these costs and the expected revenue that you'll be getting once you start up your business. Whatever is left after you cover costs with available investment funds and revenue is the approximate amount of funding that you require. As far as estimating revenue, you can benchmark against industry counterparts, while giving room for fluctuations and bad months.

It can sometimes be difficult to arrive at an exact figure when it comes to estimating funding requirements. In such a case, you are allowed to come up with different amounts supported by different scenarios. For instance, you can estimate that a worst-case scenario where you made zero sales within a six-month period will require $50,000 in investment capital, while a best-case scenario of constant sales will require $20,000. Having these numbers will show investors that you have considered all possibilities, which is a trait that all good business people and entrepreneurs should have. Your funding requirements section will do well to be supported by charts and graphs that can easily walk an investor through your financials across a defined timeline.

At this point, you are probably wondering, how do you determine what percentage of equity correlates to a particular amount of capital? This is where the valuation of your business comes in. You have to determine how much your business is worth. For instance, if you ask investors to give you $25,000 for a 10 percent stake, you are essentially saying your business is worth $250,000. How do you arrive at this?

Revenue is often the simplest way of estimating the worth of a company. Many business owners will value their businesses as a multiple of their revenue, with these multiples being determined by industry. Remember that revenue doesn't automatically translate to profit, so your valuation should also consider your profit margin. A business broker can help you correctly determine how much your business is worth, especially if they have dealt with similar businesses in your industry.

Financial Projections

The financial projections section is where you sell your faith and hope to the investors. At this point, you'll be telling potential investors that your business will grow by this much and that the money they invest today will be worth that much in a year's time, or two. When scrutinizing your financial projections, investors and potential partners will be looking out for revenue growth and market trends. If you have already piloted your product on a small scale, include this information in your financial projections. For instance, you may have started with a food truck and now want to open a restaurant. Talk about how much revenue you earned from the food truck, and how much you expect to earn from a restaurant that provides similar meals to an even larger population.

If you are starting fresh with a completely new business and no entrepreneurial history to draw on, you can still put together an impressive financials section. You can use information from similar-sized industry counterparts to write up your sales forecast, expenses budget, cash-flow statement, and income projections. All these are components that should be included in your financial projections. You should also include a break-even analysis in your financial projections.

A break-even analysis is an estimation of when your business will become viable, that is, able to operate on its own without requiring constant injections of cash. Break-even in business is said to occur when a business becomes profitable or is at least able to cater for its own expenses, and this happens when the revenue earned exceeds costs incurred. A break-even analysis will convince potential investors that the business they are investing in can grow and stand on its own, thus allowing them to plan their exit strategy should they choose to.

Chapter 3: Choosing a Legal Structure

The structure you choose for your business comes with some legal and tax implications. It determines the amount of control you will be able to assert in your business and what decisions you can make on your own. As such, it is important to carefully consider the various legal structures and choose the one that works best for what you wish to achieve. There are four types of business structures that owners should consider when setting up shop. These include sole proprietorship, partnership, limited liability company, and corporation. Before you settle on any one structure, it is imperative that you take into consideration the pros and cons of each. Understanding the various features of different legal structures will help you make a sound decision as far as choosing which of these features is best for your business.

Sole Proprietorship

Take a minute and think of some of the small businesses around your city or town. That restaurant owned by the guy from your high school who got a scholarship to culinary school. Your auntie's friend who sells homemade necklaces on Etsy. The local grocer. Your preferred florist. How many people own and run these businesses? Most often than not each of these businesses is owned by a sole trader.

A sole proprietorship refers to the ownership of a business by one individual. This individual is responsible for all the profits, losses and liabilities of the business, and makes all the business decisions. Sole proprietorships are favorable for small businesses as you'll only require yourself to set up shop. The downside of such a business structure is that your personal assets are not separated from business assets. As such, the liabilities you incur as a business might have a direct impact on your personal assets. You might end up losing your home if the business goes under, especially if you had borrowed money to start up the business. Sole proprietorships also have limited capital to work with, as they cannot approach investors who require a stake in the business before investing.

A sole proprietorship may be sometimes referred to as sole trader business. It is one of the oldest and most popular legal structures across the world. If you have no experience running a business before and want to get started with a simple home business, a sole proprietorship structure is a good bet. Later on, should you wish to, you can convert your sole trader business to a limited liability company or partnership.

Sole proprietorships do not pay taxes to the government as independent entities; rather, the owner pays taxes on the total personal income earned. This is referred to as pass-through taxation.

Corporation

A corporation is a business that operates as a separate entity from its owners. A corporation's operations are usually guided by the board of directors, who are elected by the shareholders. The elections are preceded by nominations, which are guided by the nominating entity. The nominating entity can be the founder of the corporation or whichever entity that controls the company. If investors have a controlling stake in the company, they can nominate members for the positions in the board of directors.

Corporations can take loans, enter into contracts, own assets, sue or get sued, hire and fire employees and even pay taxes. The shareholders in a corporation enjoy the profits and gains of the company but are not liable for any debts or obligations. Many well-known businesses such as Toyota, Coca-Cola, and Microsoft are corporations. However, there are corporations that are not formed with the intention of making a profit. These are known as non-profit corporations. The American Red Cross is an example of a non-profit corporation. The main reason why individuals will opt for a corporation is to limit the members' liability.

S-Corporation

An S-Corporation is a type of corporation which meets certain requirements that allow it to be taxed as a partnership would be. Some of the requirements to become an S corporation include:

- The number of shareholders must be 100 or less, not more

- All shareholders must be individuals, with allowances being given for tax-exempt entities such as estates and trusts

- All shareholders must be US citizens

- The corporation must have only one class of stock

S corporations are beneficial to the shareholders in that they do not pay federal taxes, which is a plus when you have just started a business. You can also easily transfer interests without incurring punitive tax consequences. Corporations which are not S corporations are usually denoted as C corporations. C corporations are the 'normal' type of corporations which are taxed as separate entities from their owners.

Partnership

If a second party is enjoined to a sole proprietorship, the legal structure changes and becomes a partnership. A partnership refers to a legal structure where two or more parties or individuals own a business. In a partnership, the parties have a stake in the responsibilities and liabilities of the business. There are three types of partnerships: general partnership, limited partnership, and limited liability partnership. As in the case of sole proprietorships, partnerships have pass-through taxation.

General Partnership

A general partnership is the most basic form of a partnership. A general partnership is seen to be formed when two or more parties come together and agree to start a business. This agreement may be oral. As good practice, there is a need to have proof of partnership such as a written agreement which may be used for future reference and/or disputes. In general partnerships, all parties involved have agency powers, which means they can legally enter into contracts on behalf of the company. All parties in a general partnership have unlimited liability. This has the implication that personal assets can be used to recover business debts, and other partners can take the fall for mistakes committed by any party that is privy to the partnership.

General partnerships are preferable to a lot of entrepreneurs because they are generally easy to form, and the paperwork required is minimal. The partners are each responsible for their own tax liabilities, and files taxes on income earned through the partnership on their personal income tax returns. General partnerships become null and void when a partner dies (if there were only two partners to begin with), when parties agree to dissolve the partnership or when the partnership achieves its intended business purpose and has to be wound up.

Limited Partnership

Limited partnerships are partnerships where one party has unlimited liability while the other party has limited liability. For a business to qualify as a limited partnership, there should be at least one of each. This means that there is a fall guy should anything go wrong. The partner with limited liability can only suffer liability that is commensurate to the level of their investment. That is, a limited partner's personal assets cannot be used to cover business losses and debts. They can only lose what they invested in the first place. The downside of a limited partnership lies squarely on the shoulders of the general partner, seeing that they could lose their personal assets if the business goes belly up.

Usually, the limited liability partners are only able to invest and do not make decisions or exercise control over the business' operations. If a partner with limited liability takes on an active role in the decisions and operations of the company, there is a likelihood of incurring general partner liability.

Limited Liability Partnership

In a limited liability partnership, all parties privy to the partnership are answerable for their own lack of due diligence and cannot take the fall for business mistakes committed by any other party. That is, all the parties in a limited liability partnership are protected against losing their assets should the business go south. In the case of a lawsuit that results in recovery of assets, only the assets registered under the partnership are affected. Partners' personal assets are protected. The parties in this type of partnership have a stake in controlling the day to day operations of the business and can leave the partnership as they wish. New partners can also be easily added to the partnership.

Professions that involve multiple partners contributing invaluable expertise usually prefer limited liability partnerships. These professions include accounting, law and medical practices.

Choosing a Business Partner

If you decide to go for a partnership structure, you might have to deal with the additional task of worrying about where to find partners. Many people who start their business as partnerships have already figured out two or three people who are ready to partner with them. If you are outside of this lucky group, you can still select an appropriate business partner along the way by understanding what makes a good partner.

The best business partners:

- Have demonstrated skills and experience that adds value to your company

- Understand and share in your vision and commitment to succeed

- Can offer credibility and resources to your brand

- Are financially stable and not doing through financial crises, regardless of whether they are providing financial investment or not

- Are respectful people who practice good business and personal ethics

Limited Liability Company

A limited liability company is a cross between a corporation and a partnership, in that the tax obligations are pass-through as in the case of a partnership, and it has limited liability as corporations do. What this means in simple terms is that if you set up your business to be a limited liability company, you will declare taxes on the company's income on your personal returns. However, in the unfortunate event that the company has debts and liabilities that it cannot honor, you will not be personally liable for them. That is, you cannot lose your personal property because of your business' collapse. The owners of a limited liability company are referred to as members and can be individuals, corporations or even other limited liability companies.

What to Consider When Choosing a Legal Structure

The legal structure you choose for your business will have a direct impact on the control you can exercise over your business, payment of taxes and level of liability you incur as a business owner. There are certain factors that you should take into consideration when selecting a legal structure for your business. It is your prerogative to determine how important each of the factors are to you and then choose a structure accordingly. Often, it will take a careful compromise of two or more factors to arrive at the structure that best fits your circumstances.

Capital

Sometimes, you'll have a brilliant business idea but not enough capital. In such instances, you might require some people to chip in some capital, in exchange for some stake in your new company. Partnerships are ideal when you need trusted partners who can contribute to the required start-up capital. If you have enough money to start your company without seeking alternative funding, you can comfortably opt for a sole proprietorship.

Control

When starting your business, you'll need to determine how much control you wish to exercise in regard to the business decisions and day-to-day operations. If your business is set up as a sole proprietorship, you can call all the shots. If you are in a partnership, you will be required to consult with other partners before making a decision that affects the outcome of the company. Ultimately, the structure you choose for your business will impact the type and level of ownership and control that you will have over the matters of the company.

Complexity

Another consideration you will have to make is the complexity and cost of setting up shop under your preferred legal structure. In the case of a sole proprietorship, most jurisdictions have a pretty straightforward process that typically involves registering a business name and associated accounts. For other structures, the process might be a little more complicated, involving complex reporting processes and structures. When choosing a structure for your first business, it is best to avoid structures with complex requirements if a simpler structure can serve the same purpose.

Continuity

Some entrepreneurs will start companies that are intended to run for a specific amount of time, after which they will be terminated. In such instances, the entrepreneur might want to start with a simple legal structure such as a sole proprietorship. Such a structure will allow for easy and swift dissolution of a company when it has fulfilled its objectives. If you are looking to start a company that can survive and thrive beyond a certain time period, you might want to opt for a structure that supports continuity, even outside of you as a founder. This way, you can be sure that should you meet some unfortunate fate such as being incapacitated, the company will continue, and you will still benefit from it even in your absence.

Limitation of Liability

Starting a business can be scary, especially when your assets are on the line. It can be frightening to think that one wrong move in your company might cost you your entire life's worth of assets and savings. Different types of business carry with them different levels of risks and liability. If you are venturing into what you would consider risky business, you might want to choose a structure that protects you from personal liability. This way, you can distribute your risk and protect your personal assets should your company incur debts and losses.

Tax Implications

Different business structures have different tax implications. For instance, a sole proprietorship is not considered a taxable entity as the business and the owner is the same. As such, in a sole proprietorship, all income is aggregated, and the appropriate tax charged on you and your business' income as the same entity. This is also the same case with partnerships. In the case of a corporation, you will be required to pay taxes on the income earned by the corporation and pay taxes as an individual citizen as well. This is a consideration to be made before you choose a legal structure.

Chapter 4: Getting Funding for Your Business

As a hopeful business owner, you might have all the brilliant ideas yet find yourself missing one key ingredient: money. Start-up capital is a headache for many entrepreneurs, especially since not many people have loads of cash lying around waiting to be invested. Raising the right amount of seed money for your business can mean the difference between a flop that refuses to take off and a successful venture that stands the test of time. There are different approaches that can be taken when it comes to obtaining funding for your business. Some of these approaches will require collaboration with like-minded individuals who have the money and who believe in your vision. This chapter dives into the various ways you can raise cash to start and grow your small business.

Personal Investment

When starting your business, your first investor should be yourself. It is only after you have committed some of your money and/or assets to your business that you can ask others to do so. Personal investment can be made in the form of cash that you have at hand that you had put away for the specific reason of starting your business. Personal investment can also involve putting up your assets as collateral. In some instances, you might have to use some of your savings to kick start your business. It is vital to be careful when it comes to personal investment as you do not want to use up all your savings or assets, as you still need these to go about your everyday personal obligations.

Love Money

If you are lucky, you are surrounded by loved ones who believe in your vision and ability to thrive as an entrepreneur. If this is the case, you can borrow money from your friends and family to start your business. The start-up capital obtained this way is referred to as love money. The terms of credit for love money usually differ, based on the relationship at hand. In many cases, the loved ones will agree to wait to be repaid if and when the business starts making substantial profits. In other cases, love money is given as a gift with no expectation of repayment. When starting a small business, love money is an ideal source of capital as it carries a low risk.

Crowdfunding

Crowdfunding is a term that refers to the practice of raising money for a project by having a large number of people contribute small amounts of money, usually through online crowdfunding platforms. To get started on crowdfunding for your business, you'll need to sign up on a crowdfunding platform, set up a profile for your business or project, set a goal and then publish your request. When it comes to crowdfunding for a business, you'll need to incentivize your contributors with certain rewards. Unlike in crowdfunding for charitable causes where parties give out of the generosity of their hearts, crowdfunding for business requires you to outline what's in it for your contributors. After all, you are asking for their money to start a profitable business. The least they can expect is some sort of reward or payback. As such, entrepreneurs have embraced two common types of crowdfunding: rewards-based and equity-based crowdfunding.

Rewards-based Crowdfunding

As the name suggests, this type of crowdfunding involves donors giving money with the expectation that they will receive a product or service that is commensurate with the value of their donation. Usually, the hopeful business owner will determine the different rewards tiers based on the donation amounts. A $5 donation, for instance, might attract the reward of a hand-written thank you card, while a $500 might grant the donor early access to the product being developed. Rewards-based crowdfunding is a great way to obtain financing for your business idea without being tied down by credit or commitments, as your obligations to the donors are terminated once you ship and deliver the rewards.

Equity-based Crowdfunding

Equity-based crowdfunding involves receiving contributions from donors in exchange for shares in your company. This type of crowdfunding is ideal for businesses that have a solid growth plan, that can afford to bring on board one or more reputable investors. Equity-based crowdfunding usually attracts larger investors, as it's unlikely you'll get any shares for a $5 donation.

Crowdfunding for your business is the right combination of obtaining funds for your business idea while also generating publicity around your company's launch. Crowdfunding is also a great way to build that initial community around your product or service, which you can tap into for subsequent products or services and the growth of your company. On the downside, crowdfunding can be time-consuming and energy-zapping, especially when you fail to meet your goal. In some cases, you will not have access to the funds donated if you do not reach your goal. Also, posting your business ideas online pre-launch and declaring your financials for the world to see can be uncomfortable and even detrimental for some entrepreneurs.

Credit Facilities/Bank Loans

Bank loans are yet another way of obtaining funding for your business idea. Business loans are a form of debt financing. Debt financing is a term that refers to any type of funding where you owe the lender, in that you have incurred a debt with the lender by accepting their money which you'll repay later with interest accrued. Business loans have existed since time immemorial and works in pretty much the same way that loans for individuals work. Typically, a lender will advance you a certain amount of money, which you'll be required to pay back with interest over an agreed period. The simplest business loan structure takes that form, with you as the business owner being expected to make regular payments, failure to which you will be considered to be in default. Business loans may also take other forms depending on the situation at hand. For instance, you might take an equipment loan to purchase equipment for your business. In such a case, the equipment acts as the collateral for the loan. If you are unable to pay back the money loaned to you, the bank may recover their funds by auctioning your equipment. Invoice financing is yet another form of a business loan. This is something you'll probably deal with once you have set up your business and amassed enough regular customers. Invoice financing involves getting a loan against your outstanding invoice amounts. Invoice financing enables business owners to access the monies held up in unpaid invoices, with the promise to repay the lender once the customers fulfill their payments.

As a budding entrepreneur, you'll probably only need a standard term-loan to boost your start-up capital. Getting your ducks in a row is crucial if you hope to impress your bank enough to give you a loan. One of the main things you'll need to do before applying for a business loan is to accurately, and to the best of your ability, determine the start-up costs of your business. It is unlikely that you'll get a loan to finance all your start-up costs, so you must be certain what specific part of the start-up you'll be using the bank loan for.

Your bank will not just take your word for it, so you must prepare all the necessary documentation to convince your lender that you and your business are worth the risk. The documentation you'll need to put together include registration details, your credit score, your business plan and any other information that may be requested by your specific lender. Make sure you get everything in order before finally submitting your application. Typically, your bank will require you to make a case in person, during which you should put your best foot forward when pitching why you believe you qualify for a loan.

Bank loans are a great way to access substantial amounts of start-up capital without letting go of any equity. When repaid on time, bank loans help build up your credit score, which is advantageous when you need to borrow higher amounts later on to expand your company.

Venture Capital

In the simplest terms, a venture capitalist is a very wealthy individual who has the money to invest in promising startups. In actuality, venture capital can be given by these wealthy individuals or investments banks and other financing institutions. Venture capital is a form of private equity and involves giving away some ownership of your company in exchange for funding. Venture capitalists are usually very choosy when it comes to giving away capital, and you'll need to demonstrate that you are worth the investment. Often, venture capitalists will prefer tech startups as this is one area that has constantly demonstrated a sustainable market and room for exponential growth. That being said, you can still get funding from venture capitalists if you speak their language. Speaking their language, in this case, means understanding what they look at, and packaging your value proposition to speak to this.

One of the things that venture capitalists look out for is an excellent and experienced management team that can deliver returns on their investment. This is why it is critical to include your experience and expertise in the business plan, as mentioned in Chapter 2. You need to give the investors the confidence that their money is in good hands.

The other thing that investors who provide venture capital consider before handing over their money is the size of the market. If your product is targeting a large market that can generate sales to the tune of millions, investors will get excited about partnering with you. Investors are drawn by the probability that your product will grow and conquer a huge market share, translating into big returns and a powerful market position. If you are targeting a small niche market with minimal opportunity, you will find it harder to get venture capital.

Lastly, investors also look out for your product's

competitive edge. If you want investors to fall over themselves in a bid to provide you with funding, you have to really think outside the box as far as designing your product. Your product must be unique and solve a problem in society. It has to be something customers need and haven't been able to get before, and whose competitive edge is long-lasting such that it will not be overtaken in a few years.

Angel Investors

An angel investor is an individual who provides you with capital for your start-up business, in exchange for some ownership of the company. Angel investors are often among the entrepreneur's network of friends and family and will give the capital because they trust the entrepreneur and not necessarily because they have scrutinized the business plan. The origin of the word angel investors can be traced back to Broadway theater when wealthy individuals supported theatrical productions in the form of cash donations. Sometimes, angel investors are also known as seed investors, business angels or private investors.

It can be confusing for a first-time entrepreneur to distinguish between an angel investor and venture capitalist. As mentioned before, an angel investor will often invest based on the relationship that they have with an entrepreneur while venture capitalists go into the details of the product, the business model and the potential returns.

An angel investor often works alone, while venture capitalists are part of companies referred to as venture capital firms. Venture capital firms have various ways of sourcing for capital including from pension funds, corporations and the individuals themselves. The investors constitute the limited partners of a venture capital firm, while the general partners will usually work closely with entrepreneurs and ensure the funds are being utilized profitably.

Another key difference between angel investors and venture capitalists is the amount of funding they can afford to give. Because investors have pooled their resources in a firm, venture capitalists can provide capital to the tune of $7 million plus. Angel investors, on the other hand, will do a modest $25,000 to $100,000 depending on the company and entrepreneur.

An angel investor will often give you money and then retreat the shadows where they can wait for you to sell your product and give them their returns. Venture capitalists provide funding and then stay on to ensure that your product is successful in the market. Venture capitalists will often take on active roles in establishing your company's strategy, recruiting for senior positions and advising the CEOs of the company (that is, you). Venture capitalists are obligated to provide this all-important handholding, while angel investors will do so only if they want to.

Lastly, angel investors invest in a company that is in its early stages, while venture capitalists will jump in at any stage of the company as long as the company demonstrates a potential for growth.

Grants

When you are struggling to get funding for your small business, free money is music to your ears. That is exactly what grants are: free money. In a perfect world, you would start your business with grant money only, since you will never have to pay it back. Unfortunately, the real world operates a little more differently. You might have to supplement grants with another source of capital.

Grants are often provided by the government and other non-governmental organizations and will often require you to meet certain criteria before you can be deemed eligible. Usually, the process of applying for a grant can be tedious and marred by bureaucracy, which is a factor that discourages entrepreneurs. Another reason why many business owners will not rush for grants is that there are often strict rules regarding what you can use the money for. For instance, a foundation might specify that the money given to you can only be used to fund research on how to develop an environmentally-friendly product. This means that you will not be able to buy equipment with this money, however much of a priority that is.

The best way to find out which grants are available for your small business idea is to conduct a simple online search.

Chapter 5: Marketing your Business Effectively

A brilliant business that is not well-marketed is akin to a beautiful woman smiling in the dark - nobody will take notice. Regardless of how well-thought out your product or service is you will not reach your intended market unless you execute a flawless marketing strategy. If you are just starting your first business, you might find the creation of a marketing strategy overwhelming. On top of this, you'll also have to create a marketing plan that is informed by the strategy. If you fall short of the skills or time required to create a marketing strategy and plan, you can outsource this work to a consultant. The consultant will then create for you a marketing strategy that contains your value proposition, target customer information, and ways of turning this target customer into actual clients. The strategy will also outline your company's thematic marketing messages. The marketing plan goes into the details of how the marketing strategy will be executed, including outlining key marketing activities against timelines.

A robust marketing strategy will take your company places as far as increased visibility in an increasingly saturated market. That being said, there are other ways you can involve yourself in marketing your business. These ways are easy to execute on your own and do not require you to have a big marketing budget. As an entrepreneur, you will need to internalize these simple means of marketing your business to the point where they become second nature. Doing so will allow you to naturally plug in your business in everyday situations and conversations.

Create a Powerful Elevator Pitch

In the world of business, there's a phenomenon known as an elevator pitch. You will probably have heard it before in corporate and business environments. As a business owner, it will be one of your most powerful conversation tools. An elevator pitch is a crisp and concise description of a concept in a way that succinctly conveys relevant information to a listener. An elevator pitch is a sales pitch that knows what it wants. It is called this because it should be brief enough to be delivered during an elevator ride, which typically averages just under two minutes. In short, when creating an elevator pitch, you should ensure you keep your talking to under two minutes.

There are three components that combine to make a powerful elevator pitch. The first component is the stimulation of interest. At the very beginning, you have to present yourself in a way that communicates that you are offering something of great value in exchange for a few your audience's resources. There is a trick used by successful salespeople that is sometimes referred to as the 100/20 Rule. The 100/20 Rule is based on the premise that for a customer to be willing to give you their $20, you have to be providing more than that, maybe even $100. As such, your elevator pitch should clearly communicate that you are providing a lot of value and asking only for a small investment from your customer. In order to communicate this effectively, you have to believe it first.

The second component of a powerful elevator pitch is the transition. Now that you have your audience's attention, you have to address a specific need that your audience has, and a problem that the will continue to have if they do not take you up on your offer. The idea is not to shock your potential customers into committing their cash to your product or service. The idea is to push the customers towards an a-ha moment where they actually begin to think of how simpler, easier or better their lives would be should they choose your product or service. At this point in your elevator pitch, you might be tempted to over-promise with the intention of hooking the customer. This is not only unethical but disadvantageous to your brand as well. You should always tell the truth as far as what you can deliver is concerned. If you thought through your value proposition and mission statement well, there will be no need to stretch the truth.

Lastly, the third component of your elevator pitch will be the sharing of a vision. Let potential investors and partners understand what your long-term vision for your company is, what value they will be getting in the present and in future and what you need from them to actualize this value and vision. In sharing your vision, keep the 100/20 rule in mind. You want to ensure that what you are asking of them to make your vision come true is way less than what they stand to gain from your vision coming true.

Do not close your elevator pitch on an ambiguous note. You'll need to ensure that you get feedback on your pitch straight away. Ask your audience whether they have any objections regarding moving forward with you. If the answer is no, then you have another win under your belt. If the answer is yes, ask why they object to a partnership. The answer will help you polish up your pitch for the next opportunity. Whatever the outcome, remember that most people do not excel in their very first sales pitch. Practice makes perfect, and the more you work on your pitch and your product, the easier it will be to get buy-in from investors and customers.

Leverage the Power of Social Media

Social media is a powerful marketing tool that you can use to reach a wide audience across the world. As at the end of 2018, there were over three billion social media users in the world. Facebook alone has one billion active users every day. Social media presents a massive opportunity for anyone who is looking to tell the world about their new company. The best thing about social media is that it is free to use. To get people talking about your new company on social media, create a presence by developing shareable content and availing this on your social media pages. Content can be in the form of the written word or short, informative videos that viewers can easily get through. At the very beginning, you might want to stick to sharing snippets of your new company with your friends and followers. Later on, you might want to implement a full-on social media marketing campaign. A social media marketing campaign could be as simple as setting aside some cash for Facebook ads, or as complicated as getting a fully-fledged social media marketing team on board.

Even if you are not social media savvy, you can run a simple marketing campaign on Facebook by signing up for their paid advertisements. A Facebook ad allows you to define your target audience and the intended outcome of your advertisement. You will also have the freedom to set a budget, which starts from as low as $8 for one thousand impressions. What this means is that you can pay as low as $8 for your brand to be shown to one thousand potential customers. If you refine your target criteria accurately, you can make quite the impression within your region of operation without requiring a big advertising budget.

Instagram ads work in pretty much the same way and are another area you should explore in as far as leveraging social media.

You can undertake your social media campaign directly or use established personalities to push your product or service. These personalities who can influence potential customers to choose your brand are known as influencers. Micro-influencers, or influencers with follower numbers of between 2,000 and 50,000, are ideal for smaller businesses. A micro influencer can talk to their followers about your product, and convince them to buy from you. Most influencers will prefer to be paid in cash, but many of them will still accept freebies in exchange for some bit of publicity. When picking an influencer, make sure to go for someone who speaks the language of your target audience. This means that the influencer should be relatable and possibly someone who has struggled with the problem that you are looking to solve with your product or solution.

Create a Mailing List

When you start your business, the first contact you make with a customer is highly critical. For starters, your product or service should be top notch and your customer service should be exemplary. This will convince them that there is value for money in your company, and possibly keep them coming back for me. A second thing that must happen when you meet that customer for the first time is to get their contact information. Never let a customer leave without sharing their email information or phone number, especially if they are happy with your product or service. This does not mean that you'll accost your walk-in customers and demand that they leave their personal information. Create a simple customer satisfaction form, and include a section for contact information. Collate this contact information and create a mailing list. This mailing list will come in handy when you need to communicate the release of new products, upgrades, or any relevant information that your customers need to know. A website will make it even easier to get your customer's email addresses. Keep in mind though that sending through email blasts every other minute will annoy your customers. As such, make it short, sweet and regular, without being suffocating.

Give Freebies

Everybody loves freebies; well, most people do. Once you launch your company, you might want to start by giving freebies to potential customers. Freebies allow people to experience a product and determine whether it is worth spending money on. Giving away a product you invested in for free might not sound very appealing to an entrepreneur, but remember you have to spend money to make money. A sample or a free trial will go a long way in building your brand's credibility among potential customers. Once the customer is hooked on the free trial since it has made their life that much easier, they will more likely be interested in a paid version. A person that hasn't interacted with the product at all might be more skeptical when it comes to paying for a product.

When it comes to freebies, you'll want to be moderate about how much you give away as you do not want to deplete your entire stock. You might set a grace period during which customers can get your product or service for free. You could even say that a certain product has a 50% discount if it is purchased within a particular period. Such simple tactics will get people talking about your product, and this is a marketing strategy that anyone can execute on a relatively low budget.

Word of Mouth

The Internet has made it possible to interact with people without leaving your house, but it will never replace a genuine and heartfelt face-to-face conversation. As a business owner, your days of lounging inside your house for hours on end will come to an end. You will have to get out there, network, shake a hand here and there, and get to know some people. The impression you make on people on a personal level can make a big difference in getting your brand known. Find platforms and opportunities that allow you to network with the right people, and make use of these. Volunteer, sponsor your local Little League team, attend charity events, sign up for that half marathon and be active in community forums. You meet people when you leave the house, and some of these people will end up becoming your investors and partners. Keep your elevator pitch on standby when you attend these events. Tweak it based on the audience and circumstances, and deliver it naturally and convincingly.

Tips for Creating a Winning Marketing Strategy and an Executable Marketing Plan

As mentioned earlier in this chapter, you will need to come up with a marketing strategy that will be supported by one or more marketing plans. Not all strategies are created alike, and this explains why some will fail while others go on to succeed. A brilliant marketing strategy can take your brand from obscurity to national and even international popularity. There are several things that you should keep in mind when coming up with a marketing strategy for your business, and these are discussed below.

Know Your Customer

Understanding your customer is the first step towards ensuring your marketing efforts are focused on the right individuals. The best way to go about knowing your customer is to build a buyer persona. A buyer persona is a representation of what your ideal customer might look like. To create an accurate buyer persona, you will need to rely on market research and data gathered from your customers. Armed with your whiteboard and marker, note down where your ideal customer would live, how old they would be, what level of education they would have and even what their personal interests are. You might also want to take a stab at their job title, annual income, relationship status, and their buying motivation.

When you have a persona that includes all the important characteristics of your customer, verify its accuracy by speaking to your customer. A five-minute interview will help you to verify your persona against real, buying customers. Many people do not like to spend time on websites answering interview questions so you have to make it worth your customers' while. A simple way of doing this is giving a discount on purchases for every interview completed. Once you know who your customer is and what they like and don't care for you can move on to the next step of building your marketing strategy.

Research your Competition

However unique you think your value proposition is, you should never ignore your competition. There is always something to be learned by looking over the fence. It could be that your competitors have figured out something that you are struggling with. It could also be that they have made some terrible mistakes that you can learn from. Whatever the case may be, always remember that there is a lot to learn from looking around you.

Now, when it comes to researching the competition, you'll need to do a little bit of sleuthing. No competitor will open themselves up for scrutiny, unless inadvertently. As such, you'll have to know where to look if you want more information than a Facebook business page can provide. Some of the tools that will come in handy when researching your competition include Mention, Moz's Open Site Explorer, Alexa, and QuickSprout Website Analyzer. These tools are essentially spy tools that can help you understand what customers are saying online about your competitors, what your competitors are struggling with and the missed opportunities that you can take advantage of.

Choose Your Preferred Channels

The channels you choose to market your message could mean the difference between turning your audience into customers, or losing the entire message mid-delivery. Tempting as it might be, you should not try out all channels with the hope that at least one of them works. Marketing should not be a gamble. It should be an informed effort that chooses the best-fit. The best way to go about organizing your preferred channels is to understand what channels are out there to choose from.

There are three broad categories of channels which are at your business' disposal. These include owned, earned, and paid media. Owned media refers to the channels that you have full control over. These may be your website or even your branded material. Ideally, you should have at least two owned channels. This way, you have an in-house platform that is fully yours to use as you please.

Earned media refers to the publicity and exposure that you get from your online and offline activities. If people are talking about your brand because of content that you have written and shared online, this is an example of earned media. Guest posting is yet another form of earned media.

Lastly, there is paid media, which refers to any media channel that you pay for. Paid media is a way of letting people know about your owned media, and to boost exposure for your earned media. Examples of paid media include Google AdWords, sponsored ads, and even radio commercials. The best way to approach paid media is by setting a budget and trying out different platforms with an objective of determining what platform works best.

Understand your Sales Funnel

A sales funnel, also known as a sales process, is the journey your customer goes through before they purchase your product or service. A very basic sales funnel has four steps. These are awareness, interest, desire, and action, sometimes abbreviated as AIDA. Creating a sales funnel is important as it allows you to determine what needs to be done under every step, what hasn't been getting done and what could be done better. You will be required to find out ways of making customer aware of your brand, how to generate interest and desire, and lastly how to get them to make a purchase.

Once you have all this information figured out, you will have a marketing strategy that you can flesh out with any further details that you seem fit. Remember also to have SMART (**S**pecific, **M**easurable, **A**ctionable, **R**elevant, **T**ime-bound) marketing goals that will allow you to measure how well your marketing strategy and plan are doing.

Chapter 6: Effective Administration Tips for Small Businesses

Most business owners would rather not deal with the administrative tasks of running their organizations. Entrepreneurs flourish when they are making business decisions, winning customers and growing sales. They would prefer to never deal with the clerical duties of a business. The bad news is that the administration of your business is well within your mandate as a business owner. The good news is that you can always hire someone else to do the seemingly mundane tasks for you, so you can focus on your priorities. When it comes to the administration of a business, there are several dockets that stand out as requiring prioritization. These dockets include bookkeeping, budgeting, cash flow management, and tax preparation.

Bookkeeping

Bookkeeping is an accounting term that refers to the process of creating and maintaining records of the financial transactions of an organization. In accounting, a book is a record of all the financial positions of a trader and is the inspiration behind the term bookkeeping. You should never compromise when it comes to keeping accurate records of your financial transactions. For starters, the law requires that you keep such records. Secondly, you need up-to-date records of your financial affairs so that you can always be appraised on the state of your business' finances. Bookkeeping helps you to know when you are in the red and when you are in the clear. Maintaining proper financial records comes in handy during budgeting and tax preparation. It also informs financial analysis which can give you insights regarding your company's financial performance. With updated records, you can field questions from investors and give a proper view of your current standing. Bookkeeping also informs your financial management; you will know how much you spent and whether you can cut back on spending, and how much you are owed and when to expect it. At a very fundamental level, bookkeeping is essential for your peace of mind as you will have a clear view of your finances all the time.

Many people get confused when it comes to distinguishing between a bookkeeper and an accountant. The key distinction is that a bookkeeper maintains records, while an accountant interprets and analyzes these records. An accountant's work is informed by the information that the bookkeeper has recorded. From this information, an accountant may prepare financial statements, perform audits and even create reports for tax purposes.

As a business owner, having a bookkeeper is ideal as it takes off the work from your mostly full plate. However, you might not be able to afford one immediately. If this is the case, you can enlist the use of tried and tested software to ease your workload. Some of the software you can look into for your small business bookkeeping and other accounting needs include Wave, GoDaddy Bookkeeping, QuickBooks Online, Zoho Books, FreshBooks, and Xero. The monthly cost for these software ranges from $5 a month, an amount that is well within the budget of a small business. What's more, this software is available on mobile as well, which means you have a real-time view of your financial data while on the move. You can make good use of your daily commute to update your numbers on your mobile and make any necessary changes. As invoices get paid and income streams in, you will be able to observe deficits turning into surpluses without ever needing to log onto a laptop, unless you want to.

With all financial data kept up to date, it will be relatively easy to create financial statements on your own. If you do not have confidence in your accounting abilities, there are tools to assist in this area as well. One of these tools is something that you'll probably use many times over in the course of your business' lifetime, and that is Microsoft Excel. Microsoft Excel allows you to create financial statements with minimal hassle. To create a financial statement on Excel, open the application, click on new document and choose from the templates available on there. If you do not see what you are looking for, try using the search bar to access thousands of online templates. This is as simple as it gets.

As your business grows and your numbers become more robust, you might need additional reinforcement. NetSuite ERP and Sage Intacct are two tools that thriving business can invest in to make their accounting tasks easier. In the first year of business, accounting software and the occasional freelance bookkeeper should keep your books in good shape. As your business grows, you might want to hire the services of an accountant regularly. Accountants especially come in handy during tax preparation when you have to file your returns.

Budgeting

Budgeting is yet another administrative task that you'll need to worry about as a business owner. A budget is a useful tool that comes in handy in business and in personal life too. In the simplest terms, a budget is an estimation of income versus expenditure over a period of time. There are several approaches to budgeting that a small business can adopt. When you are getting started out without much historical data to count on, zero-based budgeting will likely be the method you prefer. As the name suggests, a zero-based budget starts with a completely new slate with no figures being carried over from the previous budget period. If you opt for a zero-based approach, you have to be able to justify the expenses that you include in your budget. In the absence of company historical data, you may benchmark with industry counterparts for estimates.

The other approach to budgeting is known as value proposition budgeting. Value proposition budgeting involves the inclusion of budget items that are justifiably supported by demonstrated value. This approach involves mainly having a mindset that enables you to weed out anything that is not value-adding to the business. If you include the purchase of particular equipment in the budget, you must support this choice with quantifiable value in as far as showing how the equipment will be useful to the business.

Incremental budgeting is a budgeting technique that is preferred by businesses and companies that have been in business for a while. This type of approach involves using the previous year's actual figures and adding a percentage to estimate the current year's budget. This form of approach is easily understood and is a popular choice in many organizations. The downside of this budgeting approach is that it can easily perpetuate inefficiencies in that is it automatically expected that certain costs will steadily grow every year even though these can be managed otherwise. In the case of companies that have multiple managers, incremental budgeting may promote laxity in the sense that managers feel entitled to have bigger spending budgets regardless of their previous performance.

Activity-based budgeting is the other approach that you can use to come up with a budget for your small business. In this approach, you'll start by defining the final desired output and the activities you'll need to undertake to achieve this outcome. For instance, you might be looking to have a sales campaign to advertise your product or service. In this case, you'll come up with a marketing budget that contains all the activities that you'll need to undertake to successfully complete a sales campaign. These could include brand activation events, event sponsorships, and placement of ads on television and radio. After coming up with a comprehensive list of activities required, you'll then estimate the costs of each activity. The final output from this budgeting process will be an activity-based budget.

Whichever way you choose to go about your budgeting process, the end goal will be to come up with a reliable estimation of your income and expenses within the budget period. When starting your business, it is best to create your own budget yourself, so that you get acquainted with the numbers that will form the basis of your finances. Later on, as your business grows you can mandate your various department heads, if any, to create their own budgets subject to your approval.

Cash Flow Management

Cash flow is an accounting term that is used to refer to the movement of money in and out of an organization or business. Cash flow management is the process of keeping tabs on this movement. As a small business owner, cash flow management is a crucial part of ensuring your business stays afloat. Managing your cash flow helps you know how much money your business has in the present moment, and how much you can expect to have in future. This will enable you to determine whether you will be in a position to honor your financial obligations. You must ensure that there are no prolonged gaps between cash out and cash in because this might result in cash shortages. When you have cash shortages, you will be unable to pay your bills, staff and even suppliers.

The very first step in cash flow management is having an accurate view of your cash flow. The accounting software mentioned in the bookkeeping section of this chapter will come in handy as far as keeping tabs on your cash flow. You can easily analyze and run reports on your cash position. Armed with these reports and analyses, you can embark on applying strategies that will improve your cash flow. One of these strategies is shortening your cash conversion cycle. Cash conversion cycle is the period of time it takes for the investments in your business to turn into cash from sales. In simple terms, the cash conversion cycle looks at how much time a dollar invested in a business takes to move through the production and sales process before it becomes a dollar plus profit. If you have a lengthy conversion period, it might mean that your operations are not efficient and you are taking too long to deliver value, and thus taking too long to get paid. It could also mean that you have a credit period that is not reasonable for your type of business.

A strategic approach to solving your cash flow problems if your best bet if you are looking for a long-term solution. In some cases, however, you might find yourself facing cash flow problems that require immediate solutions. When this happens, many businesses will resort to short-term credit. Credit gives business owners some bit of reprieve in that they have cash to meet their immediate financial needs, while they wait for what is owed to them to be paid up.

As a business owner, you should not delegate cash flow management to third parties. While an accountant can be hired to prepare reports and financial statements for you, it is best to tackle cash flow problems head on. You are the best person to make the financial decisions for your business.

Tax Preparation

Most people are not fond of taxes, and for good reason. For starters, taxes are mostly expensive. You'd have a lot more on your paycheck if you did not pay taxes. Secondly, on top of paying tax, you are expected to later on file returns to reinforce the fact that you have been paying taxes. It is almost like adding salt to injury. As if that is not enough, every once in a while, a new tax bill is introduced that throws the spanner into the works. As a new business owner who is used to handling only their personal tax matters, it is easy to become overwhelmed by your business' tax requirements.

Understanding your business' tax obligations is the very first step towards getting some clarity on tax preparation. First things first, there are different types of taxes depending on the industry you are in, the jurisdiction (federal, state and local taxes) and the type of legal structure you operate under. It is critical to be clear on what taxes you are required to pay before you even start your business, and you should also be aware of how your tax obligations change as your business evolves.

For starters, all businesses must pay income tax, regardless of their size. Income tax is tax that is levied on the profit your business makes. If you have a sole proprietorship, you'll pay your income tax through your personal returns. This type of arrangement is referred to as pass-through tax and also applies in the case of partnerships.

Sales tax is the other type of tax that you'll be required to pay to the government if you are in business. Sales tax is quite simply, tax on money made from the sale of products and services. Sales tax is usually charged to the end user. In the case of your business, this will be your customer. Many products move through several stages and players of the supply chain before making it to the end user. In such instances, players in this supply chain are required to obtain documentation showing that they are not end-users, but resellers. The final reseller ultimately passes this to the customer, who will pay a price for the product or service that is inclusive of the sales tax. You will usually be required to pay the sales tax collected quarterly or monthly, depending on the state you are located in. Payment of sales tax must be supported by a report on all sales made, including the sales that were taxable and exempt.

If you are lucky enough to own property on top of owning a small business, you must pay property tax to your local authority. This is usually the city or town council that has jurisdiction over your property's location. Other taxes that your small business might be expected to pay include excise tax, sometimes referred to as excise duty, which is levied on items such as fuel and transportation. If you have employees, you will be required to pay employment or payroll taxes as well.

When it comes to tax preparation, you cannot afford to gamble with your business's future. It is best to consult a tax professional for a thorough breakdown of your tax obligation and for assistance in the filing of returns. Once you get the hang of it, you can file your business' taxes on your own. Before then, it is best to err on the side of caution. The last thing you require when running a small business is run-ins with the law, and the penalties imposed by the Internal Revenue Service are not exactly friendly; especially not when you are operating on tight budgets in the first place.

Chapter 7: Why Small Businesses Fail in the First Year

There is no running away from the fact that not all small business started thriving and become successful ventures that their owners can be proud of. Early on while researching the feasibility of your business idea, you might come across statistics on business failure. This is not exactly what you want to think about while starting a business, but it is something that requires acknowledgment. Bloomberg reports that 8 out of 10 businesses fail within the first eighteen months, a discouraging statistic that might have you second-guessing yourself even before you start. While failure is a very real possibility when starting a business (or anything for that matter) it should not be your ultimate eventuality. Understanding the threats that your business faces and the pitfalls business owner fall prey to is key to ensuring you insulate your business against failure. Many businesses that have failed have faced similar red flags that eventually led to their demise. Recognizing these red flags will go a long way in avoiding a similar fate.

Insufficient Due Diligence/Research

You've had this burning desire in you to start a beauty business. You have the capital, the passion, and even the location. You know a few resources who would come in handy as salespersons and even beauty stylists. You know there's a market for beauty products and services in your area because you've seen how much walk-in traffic your local beauty parlor has. You're ready to get started. Or so you think.

Unfortunately, entrepreneurs that start businesses without

properly investigating the market are setting themselves up for failure. When launching a brand new business, hearsay and gut instinct are not sufficient. You have to arm yourself with data and all relevant information regarding the market you are about to enter. Is there a quantifiable need? What are the barriers to entry? Who is your competition? What strategies has your competition applied to win customers? Can you measure up? If you have to take six months to do proper research on your market, do so. You might think it is a lot of time to hold off starting your business but the due diligence will pay off in the end when your startup survives the first year and a half.

Poor Planning and/or Lack of a Business Plan

Writing a business plan is tiring and definitely not many people's hobby. Unfortunately, in business, you cannot wing it without a plan. You are sinking your hard-earned capital into a business, and the least you can do is have a solid plan to back it up. In the absence of a business plan, you will lose sight of your objectives and road map to success. Even though you are a seasoned business owner, you'll still need a business plan for your subsequent businesses. Not having a business plan may also come across as lack of commitment, from an investor's point of view. This might cost you funding, leading to the collapse of your company. A business plan will also come in handy in your absence when you require your employees to run the business without you for one reason or another. Lack of continuity planning will cost your business by ensuring that your business can only survive if you are present. As an entrepreneur, you will need to take breaks here and there to replenish your mental and physical energy. Proper planning ensures that you can take such breaks because everyone else that is left behind understands what their role in the company is.

Bad Location

You've done sufficient research on your market and come up with a stellar business plan. You're now ready to open shop and serve your customers. Two months post-launch, you are still struggling to get walk-in clients. What might be the problem? Location, that's what. Many businesses that have a solid plan and business model still fail because they chose the wrong location for their premises. If your location is not easily accessible or is hidden away in obscurity, not many customers will walk in. It might be because the customers feel the journey is not worth the effort, or they simply do not know where to find you. When choosing a location for your business, consider whether the community living nearby makes up your target market. You should also consider the affordability of the premises so that you do not incur too many costs leasing or buying the place, as this could negatively impact your business. If the location is well-known for the products or services you are providing, this is a plus. Consider too the growth prospects of the area. Is it likely to become a thriving business hub in the near future? If the answer is yes, it is probably a good location, all other factors considered.

Lack of Experience and Poor Management

You do not need to have ten years of experience in entrepreneurship to run a business, but you need to know a few basics. You also need to be open to learn how to properly run a business. If it means reading books, attending short courses and being actively mentored by people who have run companies before, go for it. Many individuals make the mistake of thinking that since they have worked in a certain sector before as employees, they have all the information to run a company. The truth of the matter is that being the top employee in a company is not the same as being the owner. As an employee, many decisions are made for you; as the owner, you will find yourself making all the decisions and being responsible for the company's survival. If you make the wrong decisions regarding products, human resources, and especially finances, you will most likely end up in the 80% of startup failure. While you might be book smart in understanding which numbers go where, work on filling the gaps created by your lack of experience with ongoing learning. When it comes to management, make sound decisions that are supported by facts, and do not delegate decision-making and running of everyday operations to third parties.

Starting a Business for Wrong Reasons

Most people want to be rich. There are very few people who would complain if they won the lottery, if there are any at all. Aspiring for wealth is fine, but it is not a good reason to start a business. Yes, many entrepreneurs start businesses with the aspiration that someday the business will be profitable and they'll be able to pay themselves and reinvest in the company and expand and so forth. However, for many successful ventures, this is usually not the main goal. To thrive in business, you have to have a reason or reasons that surpass monetary gains. You need to be passionate about solving a particular customer need. You need to have particular knowledge or skill that can positively impact the market. You have to bring your best value to the market, or else you'll be failing in less than eighteen months. It is not wrong to want to succeed in business and become a millionaire, but if you are getting into business for a get rich quick scheme, you will more likely than not fail terribly.

Premature Expansion

You've started your business in one location and it's doing so well in the first six months that you are considering expanding into another location. A lot of entrepreneurs equate expansion to success, when in fact this might not be the case. Many successful businesses have continued to serve customers in the very same location that started out in. It does not make them any less successful. Expansion is not solely based on location either. It could also be in the product or service catalog. You might have noticed that your initial product is doing very well in the market and now want to introduce a few more products.

There are key questions you need to ask yourself before venturing into the expansion, and top on the list is whether you are financially ready for it. Expansion requires capital, and if the market response is not commensurate to the investment you just might sink yourself and your enterprise. At the same time, you should not be afraid of expanding especially if all signs point to a need for expansion. Once you have established a solid customer base and a decent and predictable cash flow, look out for the green light that your business is ripe for an enterprise. If you are unable to fulfill customer needs in a timely manner, you might want to think about expansion. Another key indicator that you might want to expand is if your employees are overstretched. In either scenario, you can come up with a plan to grow your business in terms of production capacity, location, product catalog and so on.

Too Little Financing

If you want to succeed in your business in the first year and beyond, you have to be realistic in your demands as far as finances are concerned. Before you get the hang of entrepreneurship, you might think that asking for too much startup capital will put off interested investors. You might also think that approaching your local lender with a modest loan requirement will work to your advantage. Unfortunately, underestimating your financial needs will only work to your detriment. Six months later when you have exhausted your finances, you'll go out looking for more funds and no lender will be interested since you have existing loans needing to be repaid. When estimating your capital requirements, consider what you'll need to start your business and the funds you'll require to stay in business as well. Be realistic about how long you'll need before you can break even. After doing the math, ask for the money you require. Second guessing yourself and undercutting figures so that you do not scare investors away will only ruin your prospects of survival and success.

Lack of Web Presence

There are approximately four billion Internet users worldwide. According to statistics released by research giant Statista, 1.8 billion of these users purchased items online. The modern-day consumer wants to get their goods fast and conveniently. While the thrill of window-shopping in brick and mortar stores is still very real, many customers would rather forego it if it means getting their item delivered to their doorstep. If you are starting a business in 2020, you cannot afford to not have web presence. This is the very first place a customer will go to look you up. Even if you do not offer deliveries for your product, at least have a website that will allow customers to interact with your brand. Lack of web presence is a red flag that many customers are not willing to overlook. In this era where there is software that allows you to create your own website, you cannot afford to run a business without a website. At the very least, set up active social media pages where potential customers can find you and ask you any pertinent questions that they might have.

Getting Stuck in the Comfort Zone

As an entrepreneur, you have to be dynamic and change with the times if you are hoping to be successful. The modern-day consumer is fickle and easily excitable. They know that they have many options to choose from and are eager to keep up with trends. It is your job to keep up with these trends, and your customers' constantly changing needs and meet them somewhere in the middle. That product that caused a buzz last year might not get a second look this year. Your business model from two years back might need some refreshing. If you do not evolve, your business will not survive. Every once in a while, you will need to step out of your comfort zone and introduce some new angles to your products, services and overall, your business. This is the only way you will remain relevant in the very dynamic environment of entrepreneurship.

Lack of a Unique Value Proposition

Businesses that have no unique value to offer their customers eventually collapse after being in business for a short while. As an entrepreneur, you have to be very clear on what your unique value proposition is and this is what differentiates you from your competitors. This unique value proposition is what entitles you to remain standing in the face of competition and a dynamic business environment.

If you are offering something that your customers cannot find anywhere else, you will stay in business with relative ease. However, if you are providing a product or service that is generic and can be gotten anywhere else, and probably at cheaper prices, you will have a very hard time staying in business. Your value proposition is something that you should consider very early on when starting your business. The value proposition that you decide on sets the tone for your business, and informs the investors you'll go after, your pricing, target market, location and a whole lot of operational decisions in your company. Any time there is ambiguity regarding a decision to be made, you have to go back to your value proposition. Why are you doing this (running the business)? What are you offering your customers? Are they willing to pay for it? Will they be willing to pay for it in the coming year? In short, your value proposition is your guiding light, which should be constantly readjusted to meet the evolving needs of your customers.

Poor Leadership Skills

As a business owner and company founder, you are the top leader who will be looked upon to direct the business towards success. This leadership role is critical and requires you to bring your A-game if you're hoping to succeed. Unfortunately, not all entrepreneurs have inborn leadership skills. You might have the best experience and financial management skills, and still be a poor leader. Good leaders are distinguished by their glowing attributes which include courage, integrity, humility and razor-sharp focus. You have to be the kind of leader that inspires your employees to work better and harder towards the achievement of the business objectives. When the business hits rocky times, you have to be the pillar of strength that inspires your workers to hold on and work towards getting out of the trenches. Your commitment and passion as a leader will take you places others might think unreachable. Whether you are running a partnership or a sole proprietorship, you have to put your best leadership foot forward. If you are unclear about how to be a good leader, you can take leadership courses, read books on leadership or get mentored by a leader you admire. If you can do all three, even better. While not everyone is born a leader, you have it within you to be made into one through learning and observation.

Chapter 8: Surviving Your First Year in Business

The first year of your business is a crucial period that can make or break your enterprise. It has often been said that the first year is the year that a lot of start-ups struggle with, as they try to find their footing in a world riddled with competition. Statistics show that eight out of 10 businesses fail within the first eighteen months, news that is not comforting to an entrepreneur. With the right tactics, however, you can go on to become one of the two entrepreneurs who succeed. The decisions you make within your business' first year will lay a foundation for success or failure. As such, you will have to be extremely deliberate about the choices you make, if survival and success are what you are aiming for. You can ensure you are still standing by the end of your first year by taking steps to cultivate the right habits around your business and personal life.

Keep your Support System Close

When you first start your business, you'll need to ensure that the people closest to you are part of the journey. Dealing with the stresses of running a new business can lead to lots of stress, and cause you to want to push people away. Sometimes you'll think you are the only one who truly understands the struggles and stresses that you are going through. While this might be so, it is necessary that you keep your loved ones in the loop because they'll come in handy on days when everything seems to be going downhill. Your partner may not have the best ideas on how to obtain funding, but they'll be there when you are nearing burnout. When your would-be investors turn you down and bring your hopes crashing down, your spouse will be waiting with open arms and a home-made meal. This is important. It might sound like a hipster thing to say, but your soul needs nourishing when you are in the thick of running a new business. This nourishing will come from the people who care deeply about you as a friend, son, brother, or partner.

Expect Some Self-Doubt

There will be moments when self-doubt will creep in and take over all the confidence you had previously felt about starting a business. Anybody that tells you that the first year of starting a business is all great and full of heaps of confidence is lying. Your first year will be punctuated by moments where you truly doubt your decision to quit your job to start a business. There will be times when you will start to fill a job application because you cannot see yourself surviving for another month. Anticipating this kind of self-doubt is important in being prepared to deal with it. When the self-doubt checks in, remind yourself of why you started this journey in the first place. Remember the vision that motivated you in the first and the goals that you have set for yourself and your business. Keep your eye on the prize and push harder. Success exists for people like yourself; it is within reach and highly attainable, even though you might have to cross some valleys to get there.

Set Aside Enough Money

During your business' first year, you'll be lucky if you make enough profit to pay yourself. If you make any money, most if not all of it will be reinvested into your business. As such, you should be prepared to go for months without a paycheck. Foregoing a salary can be challenging, especially if you were used to drawing one every month. It is necessary to ensure that you have set aside enough money to cover your personal expenses for the period that you will not be making any profits from the business, which is usually a year to eighteen months. Setting aside enough savings will ensure that you do not compromise your quality of living. You will also not have to worry about your household bills while trying to run a business. In the same breath, you should also have enough money to cover the expenses of the business for at least a year. You will be required to sink in a lot of money to establish a foundation for your business. Think of the services you might have to pay for; the equipment purchases, legal fees, and installation of certain fixtures should you choose to have a physical office…these will cost you a pretty penny. Be prepared for this.

Keep your expenses low

It is said, you must spend money to make money. Every entrepreneur is conscious of this. That being said, you must be very conscious of where you spend your money when you're just getting started in business. Spending frivolously will run a hole in your finances, and your business to the ground. A practical way of keeping your expenses low is hiring permanent employees only when necessary, and outsourcing the rest of the work to freelancers. Also, consider working from home if having a physical office is not crucial. Cut back on your advertising expenses by making the most of free advertising platforms such as your social media pages. Reconsider where you have your business lunches; your clients will understand if you do not take them to the most expensive restaurant in the city. Keeping your expenses low doesn't mean you'll have to be stingy towards your business; it means you'll only spend money where it is the only option, without which you'd be doing your business injustice.

Stay Conscious of Being Busy versus Being Productive

You've just launched your very first business. You're excited about your new adventure and cannot wait to see yourself on Forbes 400. While you dream of a future full of good fortune and infinite success, you're taking steps to ensure this comes true. So you're going to meetings with potential clients and investors, holding briefs with consultants, preparing proposals, pitching and being everywhere all at once, it seems. At the end of the day, you're dog-tired from all the busyness of the day. This busyness should not fool you into thinking you're making progress. There's a big difference between busyness and productivity, and the difference lies in what is achieved at the end of the day. If you are neck-deep in meetings with potential clients and have no clients at the end of the month, you're busy but not productive. Beware of the allure of wanting to feel wanted and needed, at the expense of your business. In your first year, there might be many calls made and many meetings scheduled; determine the value of each and respond appropriately. A day that ends at noon with two sales made is more fruitful than a never-ending day of chasing potential clients who are unwilling to sign on the dotted line.

Focus on the Customer

You've come up with this amazing innovation that is going to blow everyone's mind. Twelve months later, no one seems to be mind-blown. You invested a tidy sum into your business and you have yet to break even. Sales are tricking in at a discouraging rate. You're just about to close shop. What happened to your amazing innovation? You probably did not pay attention to the customer, that's what. The feedback you'll get from your customers during your first year in business is crucial. Pay keen attention to this feedback and then align your product or service to fit in with the customer requirements. A lot of entrepreneurs focus too much on the product and not enough on the customer. The end result is that the customer feels ignored and takes their business elsewhere. If your customer service is topnotch, customers will be willing to cut you some slack even if you're fumbling with your first product, because they know version two of that product will meet all their needs.

Build a Wide Network

However much of an indoors person you are, your first year of business will call for you to get out of your comfort zone and network with as many people as you can. As a business person, the people you know will come in handy when it comes to getting funding, opening doors, sounding off ideas and even getting clients. If there are industry networking events in your area, attend them and introduce yourself to a few people. Call your mentor and invite them out for lunch. Make some phone calls and grab some drinks with that former boss that you always liked. People are assets; use them to grow your business.

Track your Progress

As a business person, you'll very quickly learn that it is not enough to assume that you are doing well. You must have the numbers to back up every statement that you make about your business. If you say that sales increased, you must have numbers showing last month's sales compared to the current month's sales. If you are projecting a certain amount of revenue, you must produce the numbers behind these projections. In business, numbers don't lie. Numbers track progress, and they tell you if you are headed in the right direction. Numbers are what you'll take to potential investors when you need to raise capital for your business. Investors want to know how much your business is worth now and in future, and you can only determine this if you know how much revenue you've been making and can project to make in future. If you're not good with numbers, hire someone who is.

Stretch Your First Year

A calendar year might be twelve months but the truth of the matter is that a year in business takes longer than that. Most business persons give themselves timelines regarding when they should have started making profits. For instance, an entrepreneur might say: I'll give myself a year and if I am not making a profit by then I'll call it quits. Limiting yourself to one year is impractical. Many businesses require at least 18 months before they can start making profits. Allowing yourself these additional six months might be the difference between a flop and a successful venture. Give yourself some more wiggle room as far as timelines, and watch what can happen when you are a little more patient.

Make Technology Your Friend

As an entrepreneur, there are a lot of tasks that require your attention. Some of these tasks are strategic while others are operational. Wherever possible, make use of technology to make your load easier on the operational side. For instance, automate recurring payments so that you do not have to go through the struggle of paying each and every payment every month. There are several softwares that you can use to automate payments. These include PaySimple, Ariba, Invoicera and even Slickpic, which is free to use. Automating your payment process will take off some work off your hands and also make it easier to track your expenses as you can easily run reports on this software. At the very beginning of your business, you might want to keep your expenses low by opting for free or affordable software. Later on, as your business grows, you can look into other software solutions that are targeted at bigger businesses. Examples include Procurify and SAP Business ByDesign.

Take a Break

Entrepreneurial burnout is a real thing. Your business' first year will most likely be fraught with emotional, physical, financial and mental exhaustion. Whether you are starting your very first business or are launching another business, your first year will most likely be draining. As a business owner, it is crucial that you stay conscious of what your limits are, and take a break when you see yourself approaching these limits. You cannot run a business when you are burned out unless you mean running it to the ground. In formal employment, you could take a break and go on leave for a few days without worrying that the company will close down. In your business, you're worried to death that a few days of absence will take you back a couple of hundred steps. Regardless, prioritize your well-being and take a break when you need to. Take time away to center yourself; only after doing so will you be in the right frame of mind and body to run a successful business. You do not have to book a trip to Bali (remember you're keeping your expenses low) but if you can afford a Friday afternoon massage and a weekend getaway it will be much better than cracking under pressure.

Start Afresh

It is one thing to demonstrate unwavering commitment and

yet another to continue flogging a dead horse. Sometimes, even the best-laid plans do not work out. Many entrepreneurs have stories of businesses that started out well and promisingly, only to fail spectacularly later on. Sometimes, the difference between failure and success is an unexpected natural event. You may have started your small carwash business and found the first few months to be highly encouraging, only for a raging storm to pass through your town and destroy everything you had started. Or it could be that the bubble burst and left your real estate business in shambles. Whatever the case may be, you are allowed to start afresh if things are not looking up. It is not quitting; it is more like rebooting. Many entrepreneurs are scared of looking like they gave up. It is a warranted fear considering there are people who gave them money who are scrutinizing their every move. A wise person once said, you should not hold onto a mistake just because you spent a lot of time making it. If your business is destroyed beyond repair, hold your head up and start over.

Chapter 9: Scaling your Business

One of the best moments in your life as an entrepreneur is when your business finally becomes profitable. This is a defining moment for many businesses and marks a major milestone and is a testament to the viability of the brand in the market. A business that is profitable can pay for its own expenses, with a surplus being left over to serve as income for the owner and for re-investment as well. On average small businesses will typically require two to three years of operations before they become profitable. If your business is consistently profitable over a period of time, you can start thinking about scaling and expansion.

It is relatively easy to tell when you have become profitable. You'll find yourself with some change left over after paying for your business' expenses. However, as has been the theme of this book, it is best to support your gut instinct with numbers. Using metrics to measure profitability is the best way to go about it. When you have numbers, you can track how your business is growing, how far you're off your preferred mark and what changes you need to make to achieve this. Entrepreneurs usually use several financial metrics to calculate their profitability. These metrics include gross profit margin, net profit margin, and return on capital employed.

Gross Profit Margin

Your gross profit is the amount of money left over when you deduct your cost of goods from net sales revenue. The net sales revenue is all the money you get from your sales minus any returns, discounts, and allowances that you give out. To calculate your gross profit margin, you'll need to divide your gross profit by the net sales. The gross profit margin measures how feasible a certain product or service is. If the percentage is high, it shows that you are retaining more money from sales than you are spending on production. The reverse is true if the gross profit margin is low.

Net Profit Margin

Your net profit is the amount of money left over after you have deducted all your expenses from your net sales or revenue. Your net profit margin is this amount expressed as a percentage of your revenue or net sales. There is no set figure that has been universally agreed on as a good net profit margin. However, there exists statistics on industry benchmarks that you can use to measure how well you are doing as a business. A simple Google search filtered by country or region should yield useful results on various benchmarks that are often group by industry.

Return on Capital Employed (ROCE)

Return on Capital Employed, abbreviated as ROCE, is yet another profitability ratio that you can apply to determine how well your business is ready and whether you are ripe for expansion. This ratio is obtained by expressing your earnings before interest and tax as a percentage of your total assets less current liabilities. Total assets less current liabilities constitute capital employed.

This profitability ratio is preferred by investors as it clearly shows which company would be a better investment. Simply comparing the earnings of a company may be deceiving, as a company X might make more than company Y when in fact company X employed a great deal of capital to make those numbers. Ideally, investors will choose a company that is able to extract a great deal of value from a little capital.

After working out your profitability ratios and coming up with impressive numbers, it is usually time to start thinking about proactive growth. Proactively growing your business means consciously seeking ways of growing your sales and revenue, so that you can boost your income and serve a larger clientele. Unfortunately for my business owners, there is a lot of confusion in this area, especially in regards to differentiating between scaling and growth.

In a business context, growth refers to the increase in revenue brought on by an increase in resources. For instance, if a professional services firm wins more clients, it might need to hire additional consultants to serve the client. In this case, the firm will grow its revenue thanks to the additional income stream from the new clients and spend more money paying salaries to its additional employees. Scaling, on the other hand, involves growing your revenue exponentially, while only adding resources at a phased pace. Scaling increases your profit margin at a rapid rate, while growth might make a decent but not necessarily mind-blowing difference to your margins. As a business owner, you should pay attention to growth and scaling as they are both important. However, for long-term success, you should be more concerned with scaling.

Besides sustained profitability, there are other signs that indicate that your business is ready for scaling up. One of these is having a reliable team and infrastructure in place. In order for a business to expand strategically, you require to have the right people, technology and process in place to support expansion. You also require to have a plan. Scaling your business is similar to starting a new business in that you are introducing aspects that were previously not existing. You're introducing a new customer service unit, a new or upgraded product line, a new component of the supply chain and numerous other firsts. Just as you would with a new business, you will have to be systematic and strategic about your scaling.

Scaling Your Business in Five Simple Steps

Step #1: Commit to Scaling

Many entrepreneurs are excited to see their businesses grow. They want to see their customer base growing and their revenues increasing. However, not very many entrepreneurs want to scale their businesses. The thought itself is scary as there are many unknowns and usually multiple detractors pointing out why it is not the right time yet. If you are looking to step out of the shadows and expand your business to formidable levels, it is important to strongly desire the journey and commit to the process. Once you make scaling your business a priority, come up with a plan outlining the activities that you'll undertake and commit to the plan.

Step #2: Automate your business processes

If all your processes are carried out manually, you will always be in need of additional resources to cater to your growing customer base. Automating your processes takes care of this need by reducing your human capital requirements. As a small business, there are some processes you can easily automate so that your human resources can focus their skills and abilities on other more important operational areas. Examples of these processes are data capturing, invoicing and payments, purchase order and sales order processes. It is often expensive to automate everything at once, and for this reason, it is recommended that small business owners phase their automation projects. Your low-hanging fruits as far as automation goes are those processes that are repetitive and require fairly-priced tools to automate.

Step #3: Identify your core strength and competitive edge

In order to scale your business, you will need to be clear on what sets you apart from the competition. Your competitive edge is the factor that entitles you to seek higher prices and gain more customers. It is the factor that motivates customers to remain loyal to you. Your competitive advantage is what you should be focused on investing in when it comes to strategically expanding, or scaling, your business. When you put the right resources in the right areas, your business will grow exponentially.

Step #4: Focus on what matters

There are likely to be hundreds of activities that are undertaken in your business' everyday operations. However much you want to switch up everything for the sake of optimization, you will not really be able to focus your energy on all tasks and activities without losing something in between. After determining what your competitive edge is, it will be relatively easy to decide what is a priority in moving your business forward and what is not. If an activity or operational item is not a priority, do not give it too much of your energy and attention. A mistake many business owners make is trying to micromanage everything in their business operations. Some things really aren't that consequential. For instance, if part of your scaling involves reducing production costs, you should not do an entire sweep of the costs in your business to the extent that you are even looking at stationery. It only wastes your time and the $60 dollars saved on a ream of printer paper will not make much difference to your bottom-line. Focusing on what matters also means that at some point you will be required to outsource the non-core activities of your operations so that you can focus on what defines your brand. Outsourcing is a term used to refer to the practice of using an external service provider to carry out activities that could otherwise be carried out internally. Administrative tasks, accounting, and marketing are a few examples of activities that can be outsourced by small businesses.

Step #5: Build a formidable network

The relationships you foster around you are critical in the development and success of your business. Many a time it has been said that in entrepreneurship, it is more of who you know and less of what you know. While this may be debatable depending on your school of thought, it is easy to see that having business mentors and potential investors within your network gives you a leg up on someone who does not. Your network is going to play an important role in getting the word out about your products and services. When you begin to grow and scale, you need the formidable force of a strong, solid network that is interested and invested in seeing you succeed.

Signs that Your Business is Not Ready for Scaling

Sometimes, the signs that you are not ready for scaling are more pronounced and easy to spot. As a business owner, you need to know the signs of distress to look out for, especially if you are considering growth and scaling as a near future goal. If your business experiences any of the following signs, you'll need to hold off the scaling until further notice:

Lack of confidence in your revenue model

A revenue model is a component of the business model, and specifically outlines your revenue sources, value to offer and even how to price your value. A revenue model that is predictive in nature allows you to anticipate revenue and plan accordingly. For instance, if you know that out of every 50 sales calls, you get one client paying $100 for a service, you'll easily determine how many calls you need to make to earn $1000. If you are able to isolate such metrics in your revenue streams, it is likely that you are ready for growth. If you are not sure about certain details of your revenue model, you might want to hold off until you are one hundred percent certain.

A fledgling accounting system and inability to forecast your cash flow

So, you have been serving 500 customers since inception and you want to grow your business to serve 300 more. Logically, this means that you will incur more variable costs in a bid to produce the additional 300 or more units. Can you forecast how higher your costs will be if you grow to 800 customers? If your answer is no, you are not ready for scaling. A company that is ready for growth will have a strong accounting system that has their actual and forecasted numbers in place. This kind of clarity will enable you to plan accordingly for your growth and expansion.

Uncertainty about your brand and vision

You've started your business and have been performing decently over the course of three years. You feel like you are ready to scale, except for the niggling feeling at the back of your head. You no longer feel excited about your brand or your vision. You have found yourself constantly questioning your business' ethos. What to do? Scaling should never be undertaken against a backdrop of fear and doubt. You have to be certain of your brand, your vision and mission, and your ethos, before you can replicate this on a larger scale. If you need some time out to reaffirm what you knew and believed about your brand when you started it, do so. If the end result is still uncertainty, there's nothing wrong about getting back to the drawing board. Many entrepreneurs have had to start over when they realized they were on the wrong path.

Too Much on Your In-tray

Scaling is almost like starting a new business all over again. You have to commit to the process and put it many hours of your time. If you are dealing with numerous commitments (even personal ones), you are probably not ready to start scaling. Hold off until you can give your full and undivided attention to this most-important period.

Chapter 10: Best Practices for Small Businesses

Sometimes as a business owner, you'll need a quick feel of how well you are performing as a small business. This chapter outlines several practices that are considered the most effective when it comes to running a small business. Over time, you can check to see how you are performing against industry standards and re-adjust accordingly. The practices are grouped alphabetically for ease of reference.

Accounting

Accounting is one of the most crucial aspects of your small business. This docket helps you track your money at all times. It shows what is coming in, what is going out, what you owe and what is owed to you. Flaws in the accounting docket can have a detrimental impact on your business as a whole. There are several best practices that you should adopt in accounting:

- Whatever your professional background is, ensure you familiarize yourself with the different financial statements to the extent of being able to interpret them in the context of your business

- Separate your business' finances from your personal finances

- Automate repetitive tasks such as payments and invoicing

- Make only essential purchases, even after you start making a profit

- Implement necessary controls to curb wastage, fraud, and errors

- Pay your bills on time

- Define a schedule for closing your books and stick to it

- Pay your taxes on time

- Monitor your cash flow and especially the accounts receivables

- Hire a reputable accountant or accounting firm to help with the heavy lifting

Automation

Automation is one of those exciting buzzwords that many entrepreneurs love to talk about. In a bid to keep up with the Joneses, many entrepreneurs have found themselves approaching automation the wrong way. Just because your competition has automated certain processes doesn't mean you should rush to replicate that automation in your operations. These are the best practices you should have in mind when you start to think of automating your small business processes:

- Start slowly by automating the non-critical processes and then build up to the customer-centric processes

- Choose the right automation tools that are in line with your business goals as far as capabilities and scalability are concerned

- Set goals that will help you determine the success and return on investment of the automation

- Manage your various stakeholders and their stakeholder behaviors by defining process owners and involving your staff in the automation process

- Train your users on the automated process

- Make automation a continuous improvement process rather than a one-off project

- Have a back-up plan to ensure your process continue uninterrupted in the event of technology glitches

Branding

When it comes to branding, the message you want to send out there is one of coherence and uniformity. Whatever message you send through your social media pages should be replicated on your website. Identify your marketing themes and messages and share them appropriately on your various channels. The message should remain similar across all channels. The only changes to be made should be those that tailor the marketing message in a way that allows the message to be easily consumed on a particular channel.

Benchmarking

Seeing as you will not be operating in a vacuum, it is always important to pause and see what other industry players are doing. If you are struggling in some areas, you can borrow the practices applied by counterparts who seem to have figured out how to solve the problem. As a small business owner, these are the best practices you should keep in mind when benchmarking:

- Start as early as possible so that you can come up with a road map soonest possible

- Phase your benchmarking activities and have timelines defining when you should implement your findings

- Choose competitors who are most similar to your company in terms of size, industry, business model, etc.

- At the same time, challenge yourself by looking outside your industry for companies who have figured out processes that you are struggling with

- Define your benchmarking metrics so that you can be in a position to compare apples to apples

- Keep in mind that the only way you'll change your company's metrics to measure up with the competitors is by improving your operations and not mulling over the statistics and feeling bad about your performance

Contract Management

The contracts you prepare for your business transactions can make or break you. If you are coming from an environment where word of mouth was considered a sufficient form of agreement, you might find the process of preparing contracts nerve-wracking. Whatever you do, never engage in a business relationship that is not supported by a contract. This might be the very relationship that takes you to the cleaners. To ensure that you are legally protected at all times:

- Determine which contract templates to use by checking what standard forms are available and passing these through a legal specialist or lawyer

- Avail these standard templates across your organization

- Standardize the negotiation process so all staff know what is expected

- Make use of contract management software to reduce workload and repetitive tasks

- Have a central repository for all your contract documents

Customer Service

You could have the best product in the market but if your customer service is lacking your potential clients will run the opposite direction. Key to getting your customer service right is treating your employees as your first customer. It has been said before that once you treat your employees well they are able to treat your customers even better. Prioritizing your employees as customers means creating and supporting a culture that prioritizes employee welfare. Another best practice in customer service is drafting customer service standards that your employees are supposed to abide by when serving customers. Having a clear document that acts as a guideline and sets expectations means that there is no room left for ambiguity.

Many businesses are focused on impressing the customer during the sale and forget the very important after-sale period which can make or break a customer's loyalty. A best practice in customer service is to follow up with your customer after they have already made a purchase. It could be simply to thank them for the purchase or get their feedback on the same. Whatever the reason may be, it shows your customer that you care about them even after they have already spent their money on your product.

Data and Decisions

As much as possible, small business owners should always rely on data to back up their decisions. Data-driven decision making is beneficial in many ways, including enabling entrepreneurs and management teams to approach decisions rationally instead of relying merely on past experience or gut instinct. The data you gather along the various steps of your business operations is an asset that should be used for the good of your company.

Efficiency vs. Effectiveness

It is often easy to confuse efficiency with effectiveness. This is a confusion that many business owners face, especially in application. To illustrate this difference in the simplest way possible, efficiency is doing things right while effectiveness is doing the right things. As a business owner, you want to ensure that you have struck a balance between efficiency and effectiveness. This is the best way to ensure that you get high returns on your investment and reduce your costs, for instance.

There are several ways you can make your business more efficient. The very first thing you need to do is identify what is inefficient, that is, what is not working right. To identify inefficiencies in your business, you can start by taking baseline measurements across factors such as customer satisfaction scores, hours spent in meetings, delivery times and even administrative expenses. These measurements will give you an indication of where you should be looking for inefficiencies. After determining that a process is indeed inefficient, you should then start looking for its root cause.

Giving your customers power in their hands is another way of making your business more efficient. If you run a travel agent business, allowing customers to create their own itinerary where possible is a form of giving them power. It ensures that part of the process is handed over to the customer to do it just right, as they want to, and frees you up to focus on other aspects of the customer experience. On the other hand, you can improve effectiveness in your business by listening to your customer and providing the right quality of products and services.

Feedback

As your business grows, you might not always be available to take charge of all the daily operations. At the same time, you want to keep your finger on the pulse of things so that you do not lose touch with an entity you created in the first place. In such circumstances, it is necessary to solicit feedback from your team so that you know which areas are inefficient and could use improvement. Feedback from your customers is also highly valuable, as it helps you know whether you are meeting the customers' needs from the horse's mouth.

Growth Hacking

Growth hacking is a term that refers to the strategies that a start-up employs to ensure massive growth within a short time and on a limited budget. The expected outcome of growth hacking is to gain as many customers as possible without breaking the bank. Often times, growth hacking takes the form of content and product marketing and advertising. It utilizes readily available and often free-to-use channels such as blogs, podcasts, social media, search engine optimization, affiliate marketing, and even referrals. A growth hacker differs from the traditional marketer in that the growth hacker is inspired by a singular goal, and that is to grow a business rapidly to the best of their human ability.

Meetings and Conferences

The truth is that while millions of meetings are held across the world every month, at least half of those could be emails. You might probably have experienced it at your workplace: your boss gets agitated about something and calls for a meeting. Or your colleague who's excited about something they have achieved calls for a meeting to gloat. So there you are, seated in the meeting room and wondering why this information you're hearing now could not be shared in an email. This is the kind of inefficiency that you do not want to replicate in your new company. As far as meetings go, keep the following in mind:

- Adopt collaboration tools such as Slack, Microsoft Teams and Asana that reduce the need for meetings
- Meet only if it creates value
- Plan for the meeting in advance and circulate an agenda
- Do not deviate from the meeting's agenda
- Ensure everyone understands that they are required to show up on time

Outsourcing

Business process outsourcing can be focused on either back-end operations or customer-facing functions such as marketing. Whichever function you choose to hand over to a third-party, it is necessary to ensure that you do it correctly. For starters, it is important to determine what function is safe to outsource and what should be performed in-house. As an initial cut off, all core activities of a business are performed in-house. If you are a manufacturing company, you cannot afford to outsource the production process. Anything else that is non-core is up for grabs. Make sure you select a trustworthy third-party and train them well on how you like certain things to be done. Just because you have outsourced does not mean you have given up all say in the matter. It is important that the vendor is attuned to your brand's vision and mission.

Processes

Always document your processes, showing clearly all the steps involve from beginning to end, and the roles played by the process owners. When processes are documented, it makes it easier for new employees to be on-boarded, and for existing employees to refer to the documents in the event of ambiguity. Undocumented processes contribute to significant time wastage in many small businesses.

Payroll

In the beginning, your company will have very few people on its payroll, if at all. As you grow and onboard more employees, you'll need to make sure that you are handling the payroll process correctly. One of the things you'll need to do is ensure that your employees clearly understand what their salaries are. During onboarding, provide your new staff with information on how their net pay is arrived at, when it is paid and how vacation days are calculated.

Automate your payroll process so that you do not have to invest your energy in repetitive manual tasks. If you are lacking the budget to automate your payroll process, you can make use of free payroll software. Many providers will allow you a free version of their payroll software as long as you have a limited number of employees. Examples of free payroll software include TimeTrex, HR.my, and Payroll4Free.com.

Record-Keeping

Keep your records well-organized and up-to-date to ensure that you can always access information whenever you need it. Documents are an essential part of your business, whether they are printed or electronic. It is also important to come up with a document management policy so that you can communicate your company's preferred organization, storage, and disposal practices.

Regulatory Awareness

It's probably the last thing you want to think about as an entrepreneur, but you should be up to date with any legal changes affecting your business. If you are not keen on getting embroiled in the legalese, always consult an attorney to break down the laws for you.

Social Media

Whether you run an online business or operate a physical store social media will eventually become a part of your business. Seeing as this is your predicament, the best you can do is ensure that you know how to deal with social media as a component of your commercial activities. Here are some key things to remember:

- Hire a social media manager--you'll probably not have the time to engage everyone across all social media platforms on top of ensuring your social media marketing activities are on time

- Be careful of what your brand endorses or appears to endorse; the Internet requires careful navigation and one wrong move could bring your brand crashing down

Software

As your business grows, you'll probably want to invest in software that is robust and that which supports your scaling aspirations. With so many software solutions available in the market, it can be tempting to delegate the selection process to a more knowledgeable party instead of dealing with it yourself. Unfortunately, you'll learn early on that delegating the important tasks in your small business will often times leave you in a mess, especially when you are just getting started. You need to get things right in the early days otherwise you'll spend your teething months fixing problems that you could have avoided.

When selecting software, have a clear picture of what your needs are and how each of the software options you have provide a solution for these. Software salesmen can be very convincing, and your confusion will be magnified when you are not clear on what you need.

Buy software that is suited for your industry, so that you can get all the components you need. If you are in the manufacturing industry, do not try to integrate tools that are best suited for the service industry. Another best practice to keep in mind is to integrate software in your operations over-time instead of adopting a big bang approach. Big bang implementation is whereby you replace your existing enterprise resource planning system with a completely new one all at the same time. It is a direct contrast to the phased approach where you stagger your roll-outs.

Chapter 11: Essential Soft Skills for Successful Entrepreneurs

As a business owner, you will need more than your technical skills to succeed. Yes, it's crucial to understand how the important parts of your business work, but you are more likely to exert more influence if you have the right soft skills. Building up your soft skills is how you are going to win investors, clients, and employees. So, what exactly should you have under your belt as far as soft skills are concerned?

Leadership Skills

The phrase leadership skills has been used so many times when talking to entrepreneurs that it somehow lost its impact. And truth be told, many entrepreneurs believe they are leaders already. After all, they came up with an idea and saw it to action. Unfortunately, this is not what leadership is about. You might be a market leader and still lack the essential leadership skills required to motivate your staff. A good leader is one who understands the human side of the people they interact with. They are able to cut through the boardroom talk and appeal to the emotional side of people. A strong leader inspires and leads from the front. They are not afraid to lead and serve at the same time. Excellent leaders take time to listen before they offer their opinion. They disagree respectfully and with reason, not for the sake of asserting their authority.

Some people seem to have a knack for leadership. Others require a little more motivation. If you are struggling with building up your confidence as a leader, you should take steps to ensure this doesn't cause the downfall of your business. You can train yourself to become a better leader by motivating yourself to acknowledge your achievements and abilities, and the opportunity you have been presented with to become a role model. If this fails, you can enlist the help of a leadership coach who will help you decide what your leadership style is and how you can improve upon it.

Time Management

You've gone from being employed and probably having someone (your boss) plan your time to being your own boss and accounting for your time to no one else but you. Sounds a little overwhelming, right? Right. It the beginning, you'll probably be excited about being your own boss and getting to choose what you'll do and when. It will be an exciting concept until you realize that you have achieved very little at the end of the day. You will probably have spent hours in meetings, hours chasing after clients and even more hours figuring out the administrative details. Sooner rather than later, you'll realize that time management is a skill that you need to have if you wish to succeed in business.

Some simple tips you can use to manage your time better is ensuring that you do not get bogged down by calls and emails. Constantly refreshing your email is surprisingly one of the top time wasters. Answering all phone calls will leave you with very little time to manage your business. Take stock of all your daily activities and notice where you spent a lot of time yet didn't create any value. Cut out all non-value adding activities and learn to say no a little bit more.

Communication

The way you communicate can cost you friends and win you enemies. As an entrepreneur, your communication style is the very first impression you make, and you know what they say—you do not get a second chance to make a first impression. Communication is not just the way you speak to a group of investors gathered in a boardroom. It is also the way you listen, write and present. If you are a good communicator, you will have a very easy time passing your brand message to the audience.

- Here are some tips on how to become a better communicator:
- Always figure out the message you want to pass across beforehand
- Speak clearly and concisely
- Stay respectful of different cultural environments
- Observe email etiquette
- Listen before answering—never interrupt unless the building is on fire
- Mind your body language
- Embrace differences in opinion without being argumentative—it is okay to not agree on some things

Flexibility

Most successful entrepreneurs are strong-willed persons with strong convictions about certain matters. However, they are also quick to adapt to changing circumstances because they understand that it is what they need to do to survive. As an entrepreneur, you have to be willing to be agile in your thought process and decisions, otherwise, you will be left behind. If something does not go as planned, change direction and see what happens. If the market doesn't respond as you had hoped, understand the reasons and strategize. Change is as good as rest, and if you're not willing to change you'll be one very tired entrepreneur.

Being flexible as a person means that you will be in a better position to be flexible in business. Flexible businesses are able to keep up in dynamic market environments. They can respond to the changing needs of customers better and more easily.

A simple way to improve your flexibility is by engaging in creative activities that challenge you to think outside the box. You might also want to look into emotional intelligence and how to tap into it. Emotional intelligence is your ability to recognize your emotions and those of others and respond appropriately.

Problem-solving

Entrepreneurship is anything but smooth sailing. Even with a foolproof business plan and the backing of seasoned investors, you will still encounter problems that you did not anticipate. Problem-solving is a skill that you will need to have when this happens. Problem-solving does not just refer to solving huge business problems. It could be as simple as finding a solution for when your flight is delayed or canceled. These decisions will impact you and your business in one way or another. You have to be prepared to have a solution to every challenge that you encounter.

Teamwork

Teamwork is a term that is used to refer to the collaborative energy and effort of a team, that is aimed at achieving a common goal. Even as the boss, you will still need to be part of a team. Entrepreneurship calls for a lot of collaboration, even in a sole proprietorship. Even as a sole trader, you will still need to collaborate with your vendors and freelancers at particular points in time. To be an excellent team player, entrepreneurs must:

- Demonstrate genuine interest in a cause, business-related or otherwise

- Be reliable

- Listen to others

- Contribute actively

- Show up

- Always offer their help whenever possible

- Show support and respect for others

Whether you are meeting with your in-house team to discuss your marketing strategy or planning a local charity event, you will be required to demonstrate teamwork as a leader.

Negotiation Skills

In a way, negotiation skills are related to communication in that you will be speaking with the intention of getting what you want. That being said, negotiation is a very specific niche that has more dire consequences than communication. If you are a bad negotiator, you might cost your business essential leverage. As you try to win investors and clients, you will run into seasoned negotiators who have no qualms about taking you for everything that you are worth. It is important to know how to throw back a punch in the negotiation room, as you do not want a situation where everyone is walking all over you.

There are some tips that you can apply to become a better negotiator, including:

- Understand yourself, and your needs and wants. Figure out the areas you cannot compromise on, and the areas where you are willing to leave a little room open for compromise

- Understand the other party just as well as you understand yourself, so you know what they want and which buttons can be pushed for appropriate responses

- Give yourself time to become a good negotiator— good negotiators are made and it takes a whole lot of time and practice

- Attend training on negotiation - classroom training on negotiation skills are a good place to simulate real-life scenarios for a better understanding

Networking

Networking can be a nerve-wracking affair for many entrepreneurs. What do you say to a seasoned, self-made and successful entrepreneur that you've always admired when you finally meet at that networking affair? Many an entrepreneur has found themselves tongue-tied when faced with such a scenario. It is a natural reaction to be at a loss for words. It happens to the best of us. In the beginning, networking is likely to be a dreadful affair, especially if you lean towards the introverted side. However, you can still make it bearable by using some tried and tested tips that other entrepreneurs have used.

For starters, you should be authentic. Do not put on an act for the sake of impressing your audience. Speak what is true and dear to your heart, and your authenticity will shine through. Secondly, never second guess yourself. Leave the second guessing to those private moments when you are in the comfort and safety of your home. Once you are in the throes of networking, believe in yourself and what you have to offer. Be bold and composed, and let the world know about you and your brand.

The other thing you should do when it comes to networking is to be memorable. If nobody remembers you after you left the room, you have failed in networking. To ensure that your presence lingers long after you have left, introduce yourself properly and adequately. You are not just Rob. You are Rob from Company X that did Y and Z. Rob is forgettable. Rob with the drone photography company that did that one viral article with the sheep that photobombed some wedding pictures is somewhat memorable. Do not be afraid to be on the spotlight as far as introducing yourself goes. You have earned your place in the spotlight.

Being memorable also calls for effort in remembering other people's names. You do not just want to keep repeating the Rob story without remembering people's names. This comes off as aloof and will not win you very many fans or friends. When speaking, make eye contact and repeat the other person's name. People remember people who remember their names.

Personal Branding

Closely related to being memorable, your personal brand is

key to standing out. Your personal brand is who you are as a person outside of your business, what you stand for, what interests you have and the overall aura surrounding your career and business interests. Personal branding is the reason why the world knows about Apple and Steve Jobs as well. Personal branding is the reason why Richard Branson and Virgin Atlantic are synonymous. Personal branding is also the reason why you cannot discuss Microsoft without mentioning Bill Gates. These great men and entrepreneurs managed to show the world the great value they have as individuals, outside of being successful business owners.

A simple way to build your personal brand is by using your social media accounts to establish yourself as a trustworthy source of information and expertise. People gravitate towards the experts that they can trust. If you build a large community around you that believes in your credibility, you are one step ahead as far as building your personal brand is concerned.

Stress Management

Running a business is a high-stress activity. There will be days when you will be running on fumes. Stress management will come in to help you figure out how to properly run on those fumes. Most business owners understand that entrepreneurship is not all fun and games. Unfortunately, stress usually creeps on most people gradually and without many indications until it is too late. Stress management is a soft skill that you can learn so you can be in a better position to identify your stressors and wind down after a hectic day. Managing your stress will help you stay in good health, which is crucial for the effective management of a business.

Being Personable

To succeed in entrepreneurship, you need to be personable. Being personable means being pleasant in manner and appearance. Simply put, you have to be a nice person if you want to succeed as a business owner. Being personable does not mean being a pushover. It only means that you have to tame the inner voice that always has a comeback for every inconvenience be it a person or an event. Even if you do not get along with some people, you'll need to be patient enough to allow for respectful interaction. Once you get into business, you'll quickly realize that many of the people you need will not exactly be nice, but you have to be better than them. Better to bite your tongue, especially if speaking does nothing besides waste your time.

Empathy

At a fundamental level, you have to appreciate that the people you work with are human and going through a life which is somewhat unpredictable a lot of the time. Your account is not just a number-cruncher but a father as well. Your administrative assistant arranges your travel and rushes home to her baby. Understanding the human aspect of your employees and colleagues will help you to show more empathy for their respective circumstances. When your bookkeeper misses a day because they have to take a sick child to hospital, show empathy by allowing them the day without being begrudging. Say thank you as much as possible. Hand out gifts when your employee is celebrating a special occasion. These little things that show that you are human and that your employees are human, will go a long way in solidifying a caring culture at your business.

Work-Life Balance

Your business is important, but so is your life outside of it. Many entrepreneurs have no qualms about burning the midnight oil at the expense of their social lives. The excuse they give is that they have to make sacrifices so that they can enjoy the fruits later. The truth of the matter is that, if you were unable to accomplish something during the day when the sun was shining and your productivity was top-notch, you will not do so at eleven o'clock at night while half-asleep. Work-life balance ties in with time management. You have to draw boundaries about when to work and when to go home to your loved ones, be they friends, family or loyal pets. This balance is key to touching base with your overall purpose in the Universe. As a leader or boss, your employees might have a hard time coping with your work-life balance especially during those moments when they need to consult on something. To navigate this, make sure you communicate your schedule. For instance, let your staff know that you are available for meetings on critical matters for an hour every afternoon. Also let them know that you do not pick up calls beyond a certain time unless it is an emergency. If you allow yourself to carry your work home, it will be a matter of time before you have exhausted yourself beyond your limits.

Conclusion

As you can tell by now, starting a small business is well within the reach of a dreamer who commits to their dream. However, it calls for a lot of conscious effort in different aspects impacting you as an entrepreneur and as a person. Entrepreneurship is not the place for auto-pilot. Everything you do as an entrepreneur will have a corresponding impact that will either move you towards or away from success. An encouraging thing to remember is that many entrepreneurs have started with only a vision and learned everything else along the way. When you are committed to achieving success, even the stumbling blocks you'll face on the journey will be learning moments.

If you have nothing else, start with a vision and work your way from there. Look for inspiration from friends, family, successful entrepreneurs, struggling business owners, businesses that took over the world, and businesses that collapsed soon after launch. There is something to be learned from every scenario.

Keep an open mind and be open to correction. You might be the smartest software developer there ever was but there will still be someone who knows something that you do not. Be patient with yourself, and be patient with the process. Nobody has ever figured it out on the first day. Rome itself took longer to build.

Lastly, take care of yourself as a human being and individual. Your business exists because of you. You do not exist because of the business. Unlike the chicken and the egg, it is very clear that you preceded the business, and your wellbeing should always take precedence over the business. Going to work while sick and overworking yourself to the extent of missing your loved one's important days is reckless. Do not be reckless. Reckless entrepreneurs do not survive very long.

References

Agarwal, N. (2019). 8 Best Automated Invoice Processing Software | FormGet. Retrieved from https://www.formget.com/best-automated-invoice-processing-systems/

Best Accounts Payable Software | 2019 Reviews of the Most Popular Systems. (2019). Retrieved from https://www.capterra.com/accounts-payable-software/

Helpful Tips for Surviving Your First Year in Business. (2019). Retrieved from https://www.thebalancecareers.com/tips-for-surviving-your-first-year-in-business-3515786

Issa, E., & Zimmermann, J. (2019). Crowdfunding for Business: What You Need to Know. Retrieved from https://www.nerdwallet.com/blog/small-business/crowdfunding

Marquit, M., & Marquit, M. (2019). Essential Soft Skills for Entrepreneurs. Retrieved from https://due.com/blog/soft-skills-need-develop/

Number of internet users worldwide 2005-2018 | Statista. (2019). Retrieved from https://www.statista.com/statistics/273018/number-of-internet-users-worldwide/

Review, H. (2019). Use Your 118 Seconds Wisely | TIME.com. Retrieved from http://business.time.com/2012/04/04/use-your-118-seconds-wisely/

Surviving Your First Year As A Small Business Owner.

(2019). Retrieved from https://www.forbes.com/sites/allbusiness/2015/05/11/surviving-first-year-as-small-business-owner/#184edc8d8e55

The Pros and Cons of Crowdfunding Your Business. (2019). Retrieved from https://www.thebalancesmb.com/raising-money-for-your-business-with-crowdfunding-985178

RETAIL AUDIO SAMPLE

Are you fascinated with an idea of launching and growing your own enterprise? DO you with to start a business but don't have the slightest idea of how to proceed?

If so, then don't sweat it because we've got just the book for you! Starting a business can be a remarkable journey that can change your life for the better.

Reflecting today's unique opportunities and challenges, this book is filled with all that you need to deal with when facing personal and business risks and effectively explore your first year in business. This guide is presented in a simple yet well-ordered instructions, leading you towards the best way to fire up your fantasy business sans preparation, compose a triumphant business strategy, secure financing and deal with risks effectively that surface along the process

Everybody needs more clients to visit one's business, increasingly qualified leads, and more income. Be that as it may, beginning a business isn't one of those "in the event that you manufacture it, they will come" circumstances.

Beginning a business includes a ton of moving pieces, some more exciting than others. Such as conceptualizing business names. It then involves more tedious work, for instance, documenting taxes. The secret to effectively getting your business off the ground is to fastidiously design and arrange your materials, organize legitimately, and remain over the status and execution of all of these moving parts.

With this guide, you can stay informed with insider tips, usually only known to successful businesspeople, which will guide you and help you to avoid the pitfalls many stumble upon.

How to Start a Small Business in 2019 - 10,000/Month Ultimate Guide - From Business Idea and Plan to Marketing and Scaling, including Funding Strategies, Legal Structure, and Administration Tip includes:

- The basics on how to get started and creating a workable/winning business plan
- Going about funding and marketing businesses effectively
- Reviewing constructive administration tips
- Going through the fails that may come along throughout the first year, and surviving it
- Essential soft skills necessary for successful entrepreneurs

- And so much more

Starting a business can often seem overwhelming and complicated. There are so many things you have to consider to start a business, of which many other books fail to miss out on which, on the other hand, this book covers while guiding every step of the way towards success and growth.

So stop fiddling about and click on the Buy Now and see your business start and grow and lead you towards fortune and success

www.ingramcontent.com/pod-product-compliance
Ingram Content Group UK Ltd.
Pitfield, Milton Keynes, MK11 3LW, UK
UKHW022224230426